On Guard in the General's Chorus

Ron Cook

Books by Ron Cook

The Mountain Dulcimer

Onward Through the Fog: Short Stories & Mystery Novelettes

A Young Upstart: Contour Drawings & Poetry 1977-1982

On Guard in the General's Chorus: Army & Korea Stories 1966-1968

Firebrand: A Charles Blue Paranormal Mystery

On Guard in the General's Chorus

Ron Cook

Ron Cook Studios Publishing

On Guard in the General's Chorus

Second Edition | January 2023

Ron Cook Studios Publishing
www.roncook-author.com

These stories are works of fact and fiction. Any references to historical events, real people, or real locales are used factually. Other names and characters are the product of the author's imagination, and any resemblance to actual people, living or dead, is not entirely coincidental.

Trade Paperback ISBN 978-8-9857889-4-5

Ebook ISBN 978-8-9857889-5-2

Printed in the United States of America

This is for all those anonymous soldiers and Koreans I worked with, smoked with, suffered with, and played music with and for.

What a long, strange trip it was.

Acknowledgments

I was in elementary school back in 1954-55 when a wonderful teacher, Miss Barbara Brown, took my first "fantasy" writings to heart. Each of the dozen or so stories I wrote that year was barely four written pages long, but she enjoyed them, helped me correct my youthful punctuation, and encouraged me to continue.

Thirty years later, I was a union carpenter and tired of waiting for work in the union hall during a building freeze, so I returned to college.

I still had stories in my head, and after writing them, they helped me to successfully pass the English courses, and the other required courses, at Cabrillo College in Aptos, California. I finally got my AA degree. The next year I enrolled in San José State University with the loosely formed idea of pursuing a new trade. I wanted a mid-life career change from blue collar to white collar.

I entered a certificate program to learn technical writing. That program required me to be an English major and go through all the standard courses pertaining to that major: American and English literature, Shakespeare, Chaucer, and several writing classes. Two of the courses were in creative writing, mainly the writing of fiction. The last story in this book was written during that period.

A San Jose State instructor who persuaded me to keep writing was Professor Rew. I owe a lot to her teaching and kind words.

And there's my wife, Stella, a long-time book fan, who has also been my long-time fan. (I'm her long-time fan.) Her support, editing, and help have kept me typing away.

NORTH KOREA
DEMOCRATIC PEOPLE'S REPUBLIC OF KOREA
38th Parallel
PANMUNJOM
RC#1
YONJUGOL
SEOUL
SOUTH KOREA
Railroad
TAEGU
PUSAN

Introduction

This is not a work of fiction. Well, actually, it's my foggy remembrance of real occurrences experienced but with mostly made-up names to protect my ass from being sued. I guess I should call it a semi-fiction memoir. Or... Maybe since it's about an era, it could be an historical semi-fiction memoir. However, it's not a long-ago era. Many from that time are still around, and recent history is hard to swallow as "historical," because it's so fresh in our minds—at least until old age and drugs (prescription and otherwise) erase all those surviving minds that experienced the draft during the Vietnam era. Reality-based, revisionist history, semi-fictional memoir. Phht! Non-Fiction! Oh well, I'm not a casualty yet. My mind's hazy, but not erased. Whatever I call it, I've got to stop thinking so much about how to explain the content and call the damn thing finished!

For two years, from October 1966 through October of 1968, I was a draftee in Uncle Sam's olive-drab army. For the last 12 months of that forced servitude, the "General's Chorus" was my tour of duty in Korea. This was a real company of men and a very real tour of duty for around 40 other guys, from all backgrounds, races, faiths, and sexual preferences. We were assigned to what we understood to be the only full-time entertainment corps in the Army, housed in a recreation compound a few miles south of the Korean DMZ: the infamous 38th Parallel.

Yes, sometimes things got too real. After all, the Cold War was still raging. The *Masters of War* were still building big guns. It was the Red, White, and Blue versus the Reds and the Yellows, and vice-versa. The Communist threat and nuclear annihilation were constantly drilled into our minds, through the news, television, and especially through our military training. We nervously looked up to the sky at every contrail thinking it might be exhaust from a rocket that would cause our extinction or start mutating life, like in the movies *Them* and *Tarantula*. As draftees, our basic training consisted of evangelistic lectures on the horrors of communism, how to notice it, how to report it, and how to kill it.

Recreation Compound #1 (RC #1) was real, and parts of it are still there today. All the buildings had been constructed after the Korean Conflict ended in late July, 1953, as temporary barracks and places of entertainment for the troops who remained to police the area—troops who were supposed to have left after a short while and have handed over the whole ball of wax to the South Korean government. In 1967, around 14 years after the Conflict, those uninsulated cold-in-winter, stifling-in-summer, rat-infested buildings were still there, with a hundred soldiers on the base still using them—including me.

Just outside RC #1's main gate was the village, Yon-Ju-Gol, a very busy small town adjacent to two Army bases: Recreation Compound #1 and Camp Casey, and very close to several more. Back then it was a great place to find good, cheap Japanese stereos and cameras (Korea had no technical industry then), and an even better place to find black market and illegal items like cigarettes, liquor, dope, and sex. It was filthy, dusty, muddy, smelly, scary, and quite exciting. I'm hoping now, many, many years later as I'm writing this, that the roads are finally paved.

I've taken some artistic license in these stories to move the action along and not to offend or upset my old ex-roomies. I'm sure quite a few of those who people my stories are still alive and would probably like to forget some of the things they did in their young rebellious, seemingly-hopeless-at-the-time lives.

Many of us were away from home for the first time and did what felt normal for army guys and for a bunch of hot-blooded young male musicians and actors. As we've all grown older, I'm sure some have wondered what in God's name they were thinking at that time (or Jehovah's name, or Muhammad's name, or Beelzebub's… whatever). That's if we can remember any of those times at all. What's that old saying? "If you remember the '60's, you weren't there?" No, some remember all right, but don't want to be reminded of what they did then. Grandpa doesn't want Grandma and their kids and grandkids to know that he had to get penicillin shots all the time, or that he smoked boo (marijuana) on a daily basis, or that he dealt in the black market, or that he had yobos (purchased live-in sex slaves).

To his family, he was a soldier/sailor/pilot/marine doing the soldier/sailor/pilot/marine thing to protect our American way of life, and to keep everyone democratic and free.

Well, artistic license is not just about saving my ass from lawsuits, it's a way of filling in gaps where my memory has fogged over or disappeared. It was an interesting time. It was a frantic, dangerous, drug-induced, paranoiac time. (Yes, *it was the best of times, it was the worst of times.*") Even though our actions were sometimes questionable, and, for the time and place, occasionally criminal, it was all part of the Army package: war, sex, drugs, guns, rock 'n' roll, sex, artillery, sex, loan sharking, gambling, slavery, sex, and… well, more sex.

Yes, an interesting time. But the memories seem to fade the older and farther removed I get from them, and many names have disappeared altogether; however, most of the events are indelibly etched on my brain. (Yes, it was the '60's. I was there, and I do remember quite a bit of it, even through the smoky purple haze I was in most of the time.) That uncomfortable year of living dangerously has morphed into quite a romantic episode. What seemed like an eternity in Hell now seems like it was a short trip to Uncle Park's kimchee farm.

A lot has changed since my draftee days. I've changed a lot. We've all changed a lot. Sometimes I feel I've lived several lives, dying at the end of one, living another. Dying. Living. On and on. I've been a horseman, soldier, musician, carpenter, student, technical writer, webmaster, artist/craftsman, and author. I've struggled. I've learned. I've advanced. I've excelled. I've burned out—then started over again, and again. But through it all I think I've coped pretty well, and I've done pretty well. I know I probably should have done a few things differently, but, basically, I have few regrets. (And those few regrets do haunt the hell out of me once in a while.)

Back over there on the other side of the world, North and South Korea are still at odds. The ancient Cold War spectral ghost still hovers over the peninsula. Whereas South Korea has grown into a technological and manufacturing center, North Korea has taken a different route. It continues to defy the world by threatening and attempting nuclear testing and occasionally launching satellite rockets on odd trajectories. It all started when Kim Il-sung created the Democratic People's Republic of Korea (DPRK) in 1948 and attempted to put the entire Korean peninsula under his rule. When the conflict ended, the 38th parallel border was created. Later his son Kim Jong-il continued the aggressive posturing, and now his grandson Kim Jong-un took that posturing into a nuclear direction. The DMZ is still a wide, defoliated 38th parallel full of concertina wire and mines separating two countries that, in reality, are made up of one people. In its own way, it's like the Holy Wars in the Middle East: it never seems to end.

To quote George Santayana in *The Life of Reason, Volume 1*, "those who cannot remember the past are condemned to repeat it." …and repeat it, and repeat it, and repeat it.

Before my episodes in Korea, I went through a nervous pre-induction, a frightening induction, a lot of training and boring retraining, and an odd assignment and episode that took up the first eleven months in the army.

But let's start at the beginning…

Chapter 1
In the Beginning…

Up to my 19th year, I was pretty much oblivious to anything that was going on in the world, or, for that matter, around me. I was a pretty self-centered, slightly spoiled, younger son, in a real middle-class family living a Norman Rockwell life. My world at that time revolved around horses and folk music. I started riding at 9, got my first horse at 14, and had four of them by 19. I exhibited them at shows, rode them in parades, and went on long trail rides in the beautiful hills of central California, long before all the tech industry custom homes and fences closed the trails.

During these years, I first took accordion lessons then piano lessons. From grade school and into high school I sang in choirs. Later in high school my parents bought me a guitar that I learned to play and soon became a folk singer, which I've continued to be off and on to this day.

In 1964 my father and I built a house on some acreage my parents bought in Gilroy, California, but, unfortunately, they went too far in debt during the construction. We lived there barely a year before moving a few miles away to a small, rented ranch home on eleven acres in the eastern hills of San Martin.

That didn't last very long either.

When we first moved to Gilroy, my first year of college was about to start, and I drove my old Dodge pickup fifteen miles to register at the temporary campus of Gavilan College in a National Guard armory at the Hollister airport. The buildings were old and run down, and it looked like a very poor hick-town school. However, I met some great friends and then worked hard at having fun and playing folk music instead of getting good grades.

I signed up for the classes required for an Associate of Arts Degree, but instead of dropping out, I would just not attend and get incompletes or failures in all my classes except art, where I got straight A's. Most of my early college days were spent sitting on the gate of my pickup strumming guitar with likeminded folkies and young beatnik wannabes.

Because my study habits and attendance were so poor, I received incompletes in all my classes except for art. Because I didn't meet the requirements for student deferment, I was ripe for Uncle Sam to come calling.

And, of course, that's what happened.

Late in the Spring of 1966, when I was 19, I received a notice to travel to the Oakland Army Terminal and get what was called a pre-induction physical. That was a day-long meeting with doctor after doctor to see if you were physically and mentally in shape to be drafted. I was to be at the Gilroy Greyhound bus station at 5:30 in the morning so I would be in Oakland by 8.

When that fateful, scary, and incredibly memorable day came, the Greyhound bus, loaded with scared white boys, and a couple of nervous Latinos wondering why they were included, left Gilroy for the two-hour trip north.

At the diesel-smelling, dirty Oakland bus terminal, we were met by a uniformed corporal who walked us the three or four blocks away from downtown to an old building being used as an army medical facility. We were herded into a large room where a couple of army sergeants bellowed roll call and handed each of us a packet of papers to carry with us at all times. We were then led to another room and told to take off everything except our underpants and socks. Our clothes and valuables went into baskets that we handed over a counter to an army private who put them into numbered cubbyholes. He handed each of us a numbered safety pin that we were told to attach to our underpants. It was a lot like the changing room in a public swimming pool, at least like the one I remember from my youth in Sunnyvale, where numbered safety pins were handed out to pin to bathing suits.

There was a yellow line on the floor that we were told to follow, and as I left the changing room, I finally noticed the large number of guys all over the place, all in Jockey shorts, briefs, and a few who sashayed by in what looked like women's panties. (I thought they were trying to avoid the draft by being gay or faking it.) I tried not to stare and kept thinking that this was no different than high school gym class, but the wide variety of races, character types, and body shapes kept my eyes traveling from the heads to toes of each guy in the room.

The yellow stripe first took me to a room where around twenty of us were all told to quickly line up along the walls and wait. (My first army-related "hurry up and wait" episode.) After about fifteen minutes, three army doctors, all with captain's bars and caduceus on the collars of their white coats came in, gave a short talk on what to expect, and started the examination process by going around with their stethoscopes checking hearts and breathing and wrote some notes on their clip boards. They examined everyone's mouths with tongue depressors and wrote more findings on their clip boards. They looked in all our ears and wrote even more notes. (I felt like we were all horses being inspected for usefulness. The good ones would go to the stables. The bad ones off to the glue factory.) We were then told to follow the line to the next room for blood pressure evaluation.

We all lined up to wait our turn with the single blood pressure technician, and after nearly an hour headed into another room for the real poking and prodding.

Most areas I'd been in so far were fairly warm, but the next room didn't seem heated at all, and each of us stood shivering, clasping our arms around ourselves to keep warm. Again, the same three doctors who saw us earlier came in, put on some latex gloves, and started going around the room grabbing our balls, telling us to turn our heads and cough. Then we were told to turn around, face the center of the room, bend over, drop our drawers, and spread our cheeks. The docs went around checking all our behinds and jotting more notes on their clip boards. I remember the doctors kept commenting to each other on what they were seeing (piles, inflammation, crap). The crap guys were berated by them for not keeping their bums clean. I made a mental note to myself not to sit next to any of those guys.

The next hour was spent in the same room with our bodies being inspected from head to foot for, I imagined, lice, flat feet, bone spurs, or fungus. (Like horses, again.) By the time we left this room, our numbers had diminished by a half dozen who must have had something that garnered a 4F rating.

Now it was lab time. We were led to another room with a row of chairs for us on one side and a couple of tables staffed with two lab technicians on the other. As our names were called, we went forward to have vial after vial of blood taken from us for whatever tests they had scheduled. Each of us was given a specimen cup and told to go to the adjoining room, with a long trough urinal along one wall, and piss in that little plastic chalice.

I've never been one who felt comfortable "going to the bathroom" around others. I have a shy bladder. I just don't like people watching me while I take a leak. I prefer going into a private stall when in a public restroom, but this place had nothing but that long trough with a pierced pipe running along the top continually spraying water down the back of it.

There I stood, with ten or more guys pissing, exiting, then ten or more other guys coming in to do the same. I stood there with my hooter in one hand and a plastic cup in the other, just like everyone else. However, they all did their duties, handed their capped and labeled juice cups to another technician, and went on to the next station. I stood there trying and trying to relax my bladder, but with no luck, because more guys in other groups kept coming in to fill their vessels. Finally, after around 20 minutes, I went to the technician and said I couldn't do it. He told me to go on to the next station and come back later and try again. He also told me I couldn't leave until I pissed.

The day continued into the afternoon, after an hour lunch break where we got stale little sandwich packets and sodas and sat around wondering what the hell was going on and why were we here, until a couple of uniformed army guys came in and told us to follow them into a conference room to watch an old movie on keeping healthy in the service. ("Don't put your penis in strange places or it can fall off" type of information.) The two-reeler lasted nearly 30 minutes, then we headed upstairs to the shrink floor.

One of the final stops of the day was with a psychiatrist. I sat down to wait on a cold metal folding chair, felt my legs immediately stick to it, and could feel my balls tighten up from the freezing seat. I didn't dare lean back. There were a dozen other guys in the same stages of discomfort.

Where the other stations had three or more doctors or technicians, there was only one psychiatrist who spent up to 15 minutes with each person, so the wait was long, boring, and cold. When the interviewees came out of his office, most went through the door with the continuing yellow line that was on my right, but a few went through another door on my left. These few sashayed, or angrily stormed through, or stumbled, or bumbled through that door. One fellow I sat next to kept saying things like, "Well, that one's queer. Don't bend over in the shower around him" or, "wow, a psycho. Hope we don't get shipped out with him," or "he looks like a dumb hick. Probably couldn't answer any questions. They'll make him a general."

When my turn finally came up, I nervously sat down in the shrink's office, and waited, and waited while he made copious notes, I hoped not on me, since I'd not been asked anything yet. When he finally looked up at me, he could see I was pretty nervous and told me to relax, take it easy; he just wanted to have a little conversation with me, and to ask a few questions. He first asked me to tell him about myself, like where was I from, what were my interests, and of course, the old standby, "do you like girls?" When I said yes, I think that satisfied him enough to think I was mentally stable enough to be drafted, and he let me go. Follow the yellow line.

The wait and the interview with the shrink took over an hour. By then, I really felt like I had to piss, so I headed back to the slit trench, or rather the urinal, to try to fill my plastic cup again.

Unfortunately, more people kept coming in and I was again cramped up and couldn't yet drain my bladder. I was told that I could leave as soon as I handed in the cup, and my anxiousness about wanting to get dressed and leave kept me seized up. Finally, nearly four in the afternoon, I had to go so bad and most people had gone already that I was finally able to let loose. I thought I'd never stop. The tech guy at the desk told me I didn't have to fill the container so much, but I just shrugged and headed to the last desk to hand in my papers. At last, I got to the locker room to get my clothes.

I made it to the bus station by five but had to wait on a hard, wooden bench a couple of hours for the next Greyhound headed south. I finally got to the Gilroy bus depot around ten at night, called my dad to come pick me up, went home, and slept for 12 hours.

With the student deferment in the back of my mind, a few months later, I once again signed up for another try at college, but I signed up for only two classes, which were way below the government's education deferment rules. Within a few weeks, I got the traditional "greetings" letter from Uncle Sam. I was still naïve, even after the pre-induction physical episode. I didn't know what to think, or rather, my thoughts were all over the map. My life at home and with my horses would be coming to an end, and possibly my life on earth as well might be if I were sent to Vietnam. It was 1966, and I'd been reading and wondering about that police action over there where a lot of guys my age were ending up, literally. I became very anxious, my mother became very upset, and my father became very—well, he didn't say much, like he usually did throughout his life. He finally did say some things to placate Mom, like "It'll build character," or "He'll get to see the world," or "He'll be back before we know it." I now know he was trying to calm her down, since she was having a hard time making it through her menopausal change of life, of which I had no idea at the time ever existed.

You know, at that time, I was a folk-singing cowboy, hanging around with beatnik type students, playing my guitar, and skipping classes to be with my friends. My mind was not into schooling then, and my other interests seemed more important to me. I fully intended, if I survived the draft, to come back to my horses, guitar, and beatnik friends. Little did I know what fate had in store for me or how fast life could change.

Early in the morning of October 16, 1966, my parents drove me once more to the Gilroy bus station. Mom tearfully kissed me goodbye. Dad, who took the day off work, shook my hand, which he'd never done before, and again I got on board the Oakland-bound Greyhound along with a few other dazed and nervous compadres.

Back in Oakland, at the same place I had my pre-induction poking and prodding, we draftees were run through a quick lineup and roll call, handed a folder of orders we were told to keep with us at all times, and herded through a series of painful air gun shots in the arm and ass for diseases I'd never heard of. We were grouped in a room to be sworn in, where I tried to be a rebellious individual by not saying "I do" to the oath but was still bussed to the Oakland airport for a trip to Fort Lewis, Washington, where I began the first big scary change in my life since my first day of kindergarten.

Chapter 2
Basic Training

The government-chartered Boeing 707 arrived at SeaTac, the Seattle Tacoma airport, in the early afternoon. On board were 70 dazed draftees, including me, met by an overly friendly corporal who directed us to a line of waiting olive drab army buses. Looking back on it, I doubt if the corporal was being friendly at all. He probably knew that soon we would all be going through the hell that he and millions of other basic trainees had gone through for the last hundred or more years and was just laughing to himself about it. We waited a while until each bus was full and began the thirty-mile journey south to Fort Lewis, Washington.

Finally, we passed the big "Ft. Lewis" sign, and the buses stopped in front of a large hall and supply depot, which was the receiving center. We were met this time by what we were to expect from that moment on: the angry-sounding yelling of commands and demeaning exclamations by PFCs and corporals. We got, "all you swinging dicks get off the bus," and, "your momma's not going to hold your hand now, get the fuck moving," and "move it or lose it." Many of the phrases were new to me, and I felt intimidated by the swearing and yelling, which I was not used to in my quiet middle-class family background. I was scared and did exactly as I was told.

Once we lined up, a couple of the foul-mouthed guys, not much older than most of us, walked up and down yelling at those who were talking or looking around or just scratching themselves. I felt they were entertaining themselves at our expense. Probably, they were bored or annoyed at the duty they had pulled and would rather be anywhere else than there. Then again, they might have been natural assholes to begin with.

After fifteen minutes of verbal abuse, the door opened. We were led into a large room and told to line up in rows and columns, an arm's length apart. An ugly pock-faced Black sergeant with a clipboard, who seemed about six and a half feet tall with around 300 pounds of muscle, yelled at us (in a high voice that didn't seem to fit him) that he was going to take roll and divide the hundred or so inductees into two different platoons. He introduced the "top" sergeants that would be living with us and training us for the next eight weeks. As our names were called, we sat where directed on some highly polished benches for our orientation lecture, which started with a few words from the drill sergeants, who all seemed to go by the name of "Top".

Top, the drill sergeant assigned to the platoon I was now in, appeared to be 35 to 40 years old. He was a large white guy with prematurely graying hair cut so short he looked bald. He wasn't large in a muscular sense, but large as in a slightly overweight beer-belly sense. He was round-faced with small, beady, dark eyes that looked a little menacing. Even with his belly, his fatigues looked wrinkle free with sharply pressed creases. He wore a hat we learned later was called a Smoky the Bear hat, a flat-brimmed, crease-top, olive drab (OD) green chapeau like those some state troopers wear. He told us "swinging dicks" we would learn to love him like the father we all wished we had. He took our packets of orders and put them in a metal box. Then he smiled and snickered in an impish sort of way while introducing a young second lieutenant, who gave us a long, boring talk on the history of Fort Lewis and on how our training would progress. He looked the same age as me, but he was at least six inches shorter. He was extremely thin with blond hair in a severe butch haircut.

Speaking of haircuts, that's one of the really memorable moments of my first day in the army. After the speech, we were marched, or rather herded (we didn't know how to march yet), to the induction barber shop, a room with six barber chairs and six sadistic Sweeney Todds who roughly buzz cut the hair off each of us. My painful cut took only a couple of minutes if that.

It was while I was waiting my turn that I took a minute from my self-pity and started to notice the fellow inductees around me. There were several Blacks who talked with either thick southern or New York accents. There were white guys talking the same way. Some looked like they should still be in high school, and some looked like they should be in prison. (I found out later, several were told by judges to join the army or go to jail.) Of course, this being 1966, a few guys had extremely long hippy-style hair (straight for whites, bushy Afros for Blacks). The long-haired guys drew the ire of the barbers, who would call them queers, faggots, momma's boys, and roughly shear them until they were nearly bald. One guy took offense and started to get up to take a poke at the barber but was immediately confronted by a large black corporal who told him to sit down or spend his two years in the stockade.

After each of us was pruned and the hair was piled up ankle deep on the floor, we were all led to the supply area and lined up single file to get our new army gear. Behind the counters were a dozen or so privates and corporals, several who looked my age. They were led by an old sergeant (probably 40 or so—old to a 19-year-old draftee) who sat at a desk behind his supply crew. He had a load of bars on his sleeve that I learned later were hash marks denoting the number of tours of duty he'd been on.

The line slowly moved forward, and I came to the first private, who handed me a duffel bag. The second gave me a laundry bag. I was told that all I was to be issued would fit in the bags. As I moved along, I was given two pairs of fatigues, consisting of baggy OD pants and shirts, two jackets and one jacket liner, two pairs of combat boots, two pairs each of OD boxer shorts, t-shirts and socks, and two dress uniforms with shirts and ties, and two pairs of dress shoes. The idea was that one pair of everything would be cleaned and folded by the army's laundry service, and ready for inspection while I wore the other pair. All the clothes looked too big for my skinny 135-pound body.

Once we made it through the supply lines, we lined up along tables where we put everything except the dress uniforms into the bags, then were yelled at to get in line for the olive-drab army busses that would take us to our new homes, communal barracks somewhere in the middle of Fort Lewis.

My mind was spinning. This was the first time I was ever away from home, coming into a totally unfamiliar, alien environment, getting yelled at for, what I thought, was no reason at all, and abused like I was a freshman again going to high school on the first day. That feeling continued every day for the next eight weeks.

Week 1: Getting to know Top, the drill sergeant. Meeting barracks mates. (Criminals, school kids, spoiled rich kids, all accents, and races.) Lots of PT (Physical Training) and lots of yelling. Learning how to march, with and without rifles. Aching muscles and not enough sleep. Written tests so the Army could figure where each draftee or enlisted regular army guys would be assigned.

Week 2: Much more PT. Forced hikes. More yelling. First KP (Kitchen Patrol), up at 4, back to the barracks after 8pm, where I learned how to serve food and clean large cooking pots and pans. The only good thing about KP was eating some of the meat scrapings off the pans before washing. More marching.

It was also during this week that I got an emergency phone call from my father. My mother was in the hospital. She tried to shoot herself with my father's old .22 rifle but couldn't, fortunately, reach the trigger and point the barrel at herself. My father said mom was going through menopause and was having a hard time without me or my older brother around anymore.

This was the first I'd heard of menopause and didn't really know what it meant. I asked Top about getting leave to go home to see my mother, but no luck. Without an official notice, from a doctor or Red Cross, I had to stay for more training with that episode constantly on my mind.

Week 3: Much more PT. More marching. Our first weapons training. Learned protective moves when someone comes at you with a knife. More forced hikes, now at 10 miles. Someone went AWOL. Never saw him again.

I used the phone both next to the barracks and called my dad. Mom was fine and back home. Dad broke the rifle and threw it away. I breathed a little easier.

Week 4: PT was getting easier, or else I was getting a little stronger. My oversized uniform was fitting a little better. Our first camp out. A trip to the rifle range. I was pretty good, and it made me worry I would be assigned to the infantry and get sent to Vietnam.

We had our first outing to the PX (Post Exchange) so we could get any toiletries or personal items we might be running out of. Besides getting a new toothbrush and toothpaste, I bought a very cheap Japanese guitar and started playing folk songs in the evenings.

Week 5: Not as much PT. More hiking. More trips to the rifle range. Eating C-rations (Combat rations) in the field. Canned beans, canned breads, canned stews, all heated in sparkling clean garbage cans full of water that were placed over propane fires. Some cans had dates on them from the 1950s.

All of us had to run through a confidence course. We had to climb ropes two or three stories high, swing over pits filled with water, make it over tall wooden walls, walk along planks only three or four inches wide (and several feet off the ground), and crawl under barbed wire with tracer bullets and live ammo being shot over us. I did okay. Again, I was worried about doing too well and getting assigned to the infantry.

Week 6: A little PT, but a lot more hiking. Learned what tear gas was like. We marched into a large dirt-floored shack while someone turned on the gas. We had to march around for 15 seconds to get a lung full of the burning gas, then put on gas masks. A couple of guys couldn't get their masks on fast enough. They collapsed in coughing fits and had to be carried out.

During this week I rebelled… sort of. Top asked me into his office and reprimanded me for disobeying some order he gave. (I can't remember which one.) He asked me why I did it, and I angrily told him it was because I hated being there and was upset that I was drafted. I mentioned again about my mother's attempted suicide and not being able to go see her. Top softened. He quietly told me that there were only two more weeks of training, then I would be able to go home on leave to see my mother before my next assignment. I reluctantly agreed, and before I left his office, I apologized to Top for getting so upset. We got along better after that.

Week 7: KP again. Learned about throwing hand grenades. Tossed live grenades over a concrete wall. Learned to duck-and-cover. Learned bayonet fighting.

Week 8: Very little PT. Some more written tests. Two-day overnight camp out. Graduation. Top seemed so proud of us. He bought my cheap guitar. I advanced to Private First Class and got my assignment.

No, not the infantry. Clerk typist training at Fort Ord, California, a couple of hours away from where my parents were now living in Mill Valley. Finger dexterity from those piano lessons I took as a kid and that typing class I had in high school had paid off.

But before heading to Fort Ord, I had two weeks at home to decompress from my ordeal. Mom seemed fine, as if nothing had happened. My girlfriend visited often.

Then off to the Monterey Bay…

Chapter 3
AIT

The day I was due to arrive at Fort Ord, my parents drove me two hours south from home and dropped me off by the base office. We said our goodbyes, and I went in to report for duty. Not much later the company clerk drove me in an open Army Jeep the short distance up the hill and showed me to my new home.

Much of Fort Ord had great views of the Monterey Bay. The twenty other clerk typist trainees and I lived in barracks situated on a hill overlooking the ocean. When the January and February weather permited, I sat outside reading Jack Kerouac's *On the Road*, enjoying the sights and the ocean smell.

In AIT, Advanced Individual Training, we did not have people yelling at us like in basic training. We didn't have to rise as early as in basic training and got to sleep until at least 6am. After doing the three S's (shit, shower, shave) several of us would head to the mess hall for breakfast. We didn't have to march much except to PT and to an occasional military duty, like additional rifle and pistol training. We had weekends off and could go on leave. Lucky me. My girlfriend was only an hour away and I got to see her almost every weekend.

I was already a great typist. I learned to type in high school and could type over 100 words a minute on a standard non-electric typewriter. But the Army, in its infinite wisdom, made me take typing lessons all over again. (Put your fingers on the home keys. Now type aaa, sss, ddd, and etc.). Eight weeks, five days a week, two hours a day. I was pretty bored.

Other classes that I had to take were in clerking duties like filing papers the Army way, how to be a clerk in the field, and company clerk training. There were a few other classes I took that I can't remember anymore. At least they only ran three hours in the morning and three in the afternoon. We had much more free time to see movies on the base or hang out at the service club.

We were still required to do PT every morning before classes, and each of us was required to do KP at least once during our stay at Chez Ord. I had to do it during my fourth week, getting up at 4am to help prepare for breakfast, and not getting off until 9pm, after cleaning up after dinner. At least the mess hall food was better than basic training. The kitchen crew was also in training, and I found out a couple had been working in nice restaurants before signing up or getting drafted.

Across from our barracks was a baseball field, and several of us played ball with guys from other barracks a couple of times a week during occasional breaks from the training. I also made use of the base bowling alley a few times.

A short walk down the hill was the PX (Post Exchange, the store) and the movie theater. A longer walk, over Highway 1 and across the sand dunes, was Stillwell Hall, a large entertainment complex with a dance floor, big stage, and a restaurant. There were even a few slot machines. It sat on the top of a sand dune overlooking the Monterey Bay coastline.

A couple of weekends, when my girlfriend had to work on her father's farm and couldn't get away, some of us would head into Monterey and hang out at a bookstore or coffee house, walk around Cannery Row, and eat at one of the restaurants on Fisherman's Wharf. I loved being around the ocean and vowed someday to live by the water.

Toward the end of AIT, the barracks talk was about where we'd end up after training. We heard more and more about the police action in Vietnam, and how it was escalating. We also talked about friends we'd known being sent there and not coming back.

However, the eight weeks of AIT did seem to go by much more quickly than the eight weeks of basic training, and on the last day, there was no graduation ceremony like there was at the end of basic. A couple of instructors shook our hands as we left their classes the last time.

Then the assignments came.

Me? Not Vietnam, thank God, but the Army needed me at Fort Sill, Oklahoma!

No leave this time. I only had time for a couple of phone calls home and to my girlfriend. I took a taxi from Fort Sill to the Monterey Regional Airport.

Chapter 4
O-K-L-A-H-O-M-A

On an early Spring morning, March 21, 1967, at the Monterey Regional Airport, it was chilly and clear when I got to the terminal. Down the hill, I could see a small bank of fog stretching along the coast from Monterey to Pacific Grove.

An old American Flyers Airline three-tail Lockheed Constellation sat on the tarmac waiting for several dozen soldiers and a few senators and congressmen to board. It was a government charter with a Dallas/Fort Worth destination.

As I walked up the stairway to the plane, the first thing I noticed was oil dripping from the engines, which looked pretty dirty to begin with. All I could think of was having those engines catch fire and us plummeting to earth somewhere into the Grand Canyon. We took off at 9am.

The flight was a little bumpy, but uneventful. No fire.

The old Constellation was a pretty slow and noisy plane, and it took nearly four hours to go halfway across the country to Dallas/Fort Worth.

It was nearly 3pm, Dallas time, when I strode down the steps of the plane onto the tarmac and walked the quarter mile to a small terminal where my connecting flight to Lawton, Oklahoma, would be leaving in a couple of hours. That gave me time to get some lunch at a sandwich shop on the concourse.

My flight to Lawton was in a chartered ten passenger dual-prop airplane with a company name on the fuselage that I'd never heard of before. If I remember right, I think it said Lone Star Air. There were only six of us on that flight heading to Fort Sill. All of us were privates heading to our first assignments.

The one-and-a-half-hour flight was incredibly bumpy. The small plane pitched and bounced through one storm after another, the pilot trying his best to skirt the incredibly high cloud formations. I didn't yet know about tornado alley.

When getting off the plane in Lawton, the first thing I noticed was the wonderfully warm grassy smell, like fresh cut hay. Cattle country.

We commandeered two taxis to take us to Fort Sill. All of us were dropped off at a receiving station where we checked in.

Within thirty minutes, two of us were transported by Jeep to our assignment: the AWOL and Deserter Inprocessing Center.

The barracks I was to live in was right next door to an identical building that had been converted to offices. Downstairs were MP offices. There were also a couple of cages, temporary metal enclosures for the arrested AWOLs and deserters. Upstairs, there was an open work area, where a half-dozen clerk typists interviewed the prisoners and filled out forms, in triplicate. My soon-to-be job.

I lived downstairs in the building next door with my coworkers. Upstairs, there lived another group of soldiers who worked elsewhere on the base. I never got to know any of them.

At one end of our barracks was the latrine. On one wall was the lineup of toilets, with no partitions between them. A line of urinals stretched along the opposite wall. On the other side of the urinal wall was a line of sinks with a mirror and shelf at each one.

By the entry to the latrine was an open space where there was a full-sized pool table. That got a lot of use while I was there.

Excitement began quite early on my first week, interviewing AWOLs and deserters. One deserter, who was on gardening duty, began running through the building with a hand scythe, threatening to chop up everyone. He swung it around and chopped into a couple of the wooden posts but didn't come close to any of us. One of the Military Police who was chasing him tackled him and the scythe scooted across the floor towards me. I picked it up and gave it to another MP. The rest of my time at work was not that exciting and got rather boring after a short while.

But after my second week was over, I got a pass and headed into town for the first time. Work ended at five, and I cleaned up, changed into civilian clothes, and was on a bus by six.

One of Fort Sill's main entrances is at the end of Sheridan Avenue, a main road to downtown Lawton. Busses ran from the base to town and back seven days a week from 6am until base curfew at midnight. I figured I'd be back long before that.

Lawton, Oklahoma, is an Army town. The main street in 1967 was nearly all go-go bars separated by an occasional store like Woolworth's (with soda fountain) or Western Auto.

I walked along the street and ducked into one of the bars to see what was going on. At that time in my life, I didn't drink, having had a bad Thunderbird experience just before I was drafted. I got a Coke and sat down. In the back of the bar were two golden cages with a girl in each one dancing to very loud rock music, I think the Rolling Stones. All the guys in the room had to yell at each other to be heard. The more drinks, the louder they got. Very noisy.

Both the go-go girls were blonds with beehive hairdos, gold bikini bottoms and large gold pasties. They seemed older than all the young soldiers filling the room. One was pretty thin, the other heavier with very visible stretch marks on her slightly distended abdomen. Neither was very pretty. I downed my Coke and left.

I walked down the main street looking into several of the go-go bars. All were identical. Gold cages. Gold bikinis. Beehive hairdos. All were very noisy, smelling of cigarette smoke and spilled beer.

Finally, I turned a corner to a side street and came across a basement establishment that seemed right out of my vision of New York's Greenwich Village: a folk music coffee bar. Wow, I thought. They had food, coffee, sodas, beer, and wine. The room was L-shaped, with the bar and a few tables on one side, at the bottom of the stairs, and more tables and a small stage on the other side. Someone was playing guitar and singing familiar folk songs. The place was half full, but it was my kind of place.

I sat at a table not far from the stage, and the guy from the bar came over and asked what I'd like. Since I hadn't eaten dinner yet, I got a bowl of chili and another Coke. I was really beginning to enjoy myself.

During a break in the music, the musician came through the small crowd and talked to everyone like he knew them. He stopped by me and asked where I was from. We ended up talking for nearly ten minutes until he had to get back up on stage. Turned out he was one of the owners of the coffee bar.

All the bars and establishments had to close at 11:00 so soldiers could get back on base before curfew. I left, promising to be back Saturday night, and caught one of the last busses to the base.

For the next two weeks, I spent every evening I could spare at the basement coffee bar. By then, I was known by name and always greeted warmly by the two owners. About this time, I also received my 12-string guitar and autoharp my parents sent to me from home. I missed playing my 12-string and looked forward to playing it again.

On one Saturday night, I started talking to a guy who I'd seen there nearly every time I'd been there, a sergeant in the armor division. He was also a folk singer and guitar player. He introduced me to a private, also in the armor division, with whom he had started playing. When I told him I had my 12-string back at the base, he asked if I wanted to get together and jam.

He lived off base with his wife in Medicine Park, a little north of Fort Sill, and next to the Wichita Mountains Wildlife Area. He picked me up at my barracks after work, and the three of us headed to his place to practice. Within a week, we'd worked out a nice set of familiar, traditional and contemporary folk songs.

An officer my new friend knew asked if we'd play at the Officer's Club for a special dinner the brass were having. We dressed up in matching flight suits, since there was an old single engine plane behind the stage and sang a short set of traditional folk songs. The other private wanted to sing some Dylan, but Sarge and I knew that wouldn't have gone over well.

It might have been a month later that we were able to do a set at the coffee bar. There we were able to sing a few Dylan-penned protest songs as well as our standard Joan Baez/Kingston Trio-style folk pieces. That was the last gig.

The private was always a nervous and kind of jumpy guy and couldn't take criticism. His guitar playing was decent, but his timing was a little off, and his singing voice was not that good. When we finally confronted him, he blew up and stormed out. The Sarge and I kept playing together for a few more weeks until he got shipped out to a new assignment. Vietnam.

About this same time, I was promoted to Specialist 4th Class, which was like being a Corporal. Being a clerk typist, the ranks were known as Specialists.

However, since pay was so little each month, even with the promotion, I ended up pawning my guitar and autoharp so I'd have enough to continue hanging out and eating dinners almost every night at the coffee bar.

But that lasted only a few more weeks. My overseas assignment came in.

Again, thank God, not Vietnam.

Korea!

Chapter 5
The Mysterious Orient

I bounced back to Dallas/Fort Worth in what looked like the same small dual-prop plane that I had arrived in at Lawton. A few hours after landing I boarded a much smoother TWA 707 jet to San Francisco, where my parents, along with my girlfriend, picked me up for my two-week furlough before my trip overseas.

My parents had moved from the idyllic countryside of San Martin in southern Santa Clara County to the crowded North Bay town of Mill Valley, a little up the hill from the highly congested 101 freeway and a little north of San Francisco. After my mother tried to shoot herself, my brother and his wife insisted my parents move close to them. Unfortunately, my father still worked as a carpenter in Palo Alto and Mountain View and had to start commuting at 6am to get to work by 7:30.

Before they moved, my parents gave away my four horses in payment for their boarding. My appaloosa mare ended up becoming a champion show horse for a woman who paid nothing for her. I was, understandably, upset that I had no horses anymore. I had always planned to raise and show horses after I got out of the service.

My girlfriend stayed a few days at my parents' and slept on the couch. One time we drove my old Dodge pickup into Sausalito and hung out at the Tides Bookstore where I purchased several Family Dog and Fillmore posters for a dollar each. Another time we drove into San Francisco where we first visited City Lights Books, then traveled across town to see the burgeoning Summer of Love hippie scene in the Haight. We walked around visiting head shops, music stores, and coffee bars. The rest of the time we spent in my parents' house, in my bedroom, drawing and painting... and making out. Too soon she had to drive home so she could get back to her college classes.

My two weeks off went by too fast. After I packed and put on my sand-colored summer uniform, my parents drove me to the San Francisco Airport to catch another TWA flight, this time heading for Japan. I was on my way to the mysterious Orient.

After a tiring thirteen-hour flight, I finally disembarked in Tokyo. As I walked out into the midmorning filtered sunlight, I was hit with a warm breeze that smelled like a combination of jet and car exhausts. The smog was so thick I couldn't see the tall buildings in downtown Tokyo. I thought Oklahoma was warm and humid. Tokyo was warm, humid, and the air was thick and unpleasant. But what was that sound? It was totally unfamiliar to me. Cicadas. September was the time of year millions of cicadas chirped loudly for mates from nearly every tree.

It turned out that the next flight to Seoul, Korea, was not leaving for three or four days. The army put me, and a friend I worked with in Oklahoma, also headed to Korea, into the Tokyo Hilton.

The hotel was a lot like hotels in the USA. There were a few Japanese-style paintings on the lobby walls and in our rooms, but everything else was comfortably familiar. After checking in and cleaning up in my fifth-floor room, with a great view of the Imperial Palace and gardens, I headed down to the hotel coffee shop to unwind with a cup of coffee and a stale sweet roll.

I walked around the hotel's arcade where I purchased a small 16mm Minolta pocket camera that would fit in my breast pocket and started taking photos right away.

For the next three days, we, the two ex-Oklahoma Army clerk typists, walked around Tokyo visiting not only museums, but checking out the Ginza and the Shinjuku district, which, at the time, was Japan's answer to San Francisco's Haight Ashbury. However, Shinjuku was a little bit dicey in those days with some feuding gangs trying to control the drug trade. We found out about that later when we returned to the hotel and were talking to the Army concierge. He said we were lucky we weren't mugged.

I grew up in a meat and potatoes family, with an occasional dinner out at a the only Chinese restaurant in town, which served mostly deep-fried breaded prawns and chow mein. Bland and not spicy at all. No Japanese restaurants in Sunnyvale back then.

In Tokyo, I finally had a chance to try sushi and some very tasty tempura. My friend and I went to several small restaurants and tried something different for lunch and dinner for three days. Breakfast we had to take in the hotel so we could check in with the Army concierge on flight updates.

The fourth morning, we checked out at 7am and were on the Japan Airlines flight to Kimpo Air Base outside of Seoul by 10. It was full, but a short, barely two-hour flight. All but a few of the passengers were military. The non-military were in suits and looked like either businessmen or politicians. Two were American, two were Korean. All the rest were mainly Army and Air Force, with a few Marines thrown in.

This time, when exiting the plane, I was again hit with the humidity. The air was clear, but... what was that smell? That was an odor that would be staying with me for the next 13 months, the aroma of fermented Kimchi, and the very potent rice wine called Mokkoli. It seemed that every Korean's clothes reeked of one or the other, or both.

Those of us who left the plane and were new to Korea were ushered into a large U.S. customs facility that resembled a converted airplane hanger. There were dozens of Army and Air Force personnel sitting behind tables, and we had to line up in front of them. The passengers who were returning to their duties after having some R and R in Japan bypassed the hanger and boarded Jeeps, trucks, and military buses to head back to their bases.

At the first table I handed my packet of orders over to a young Black Army corporal who glanced at them, handed them back, then told me to go to table number 4.

A young white Army corporal at table number 4 looked at my orders, handed them back minus one copy, and told me I would be going to Camp Ross in the 2nd Division. A Jeep was being sent to pick me up in a couple of hours. But first...

I was told to go through a side door and go into the medical facility next door. I walked in, handed my papers to a captain with two caduceus pins on the collars of his summer khaki shirt, and he checked my inoculations list. Before I headed to Korea, I had gotten several shots, but I wasn't prepared for what was to come here in Korea. Because of a local hepatitis outbreak, I had to have a gamma globulin shot in my young gluteus maximus. I hate needles. I was led behind a screen, told to drop my drawers, and was injected with the most painful needle and burning fluid I'd ever had. My butt hurt for days.

I went back into the main building, where I first came in, and sat down, on one butt cheek, on a metal folding chair in the waiting area.

About two hours later, as I was trying to doze off, I heard my name called. I got up and raised my hand, and a spec 4, probably the same age as me, came over, shook my hand, and introduced himself as Gary.

Gary said he was from Portland, Oregon, and was a mechanic in the Camp Ross motor pool. He had blue eyes and blond hair, cut so short the guy looked bald. He was a little taller than me, around six feet tall, and looked very thin in his starched and creased fatigues.

After introductions, he picked up one of my bags and said to follow him to his open-topped Jeep. I eased onto the passenger seat, again trying to not sit on my sore bum, while Gary arranged my bags in the back seat.

From Kimpo, we drove through Seoul, where I took in all the differences in the surrounding buildings and people. Gary acted as a tour guide and pointed out places to visit and places to stay away from.

Around two miles north of Seoul the pavement ended and the next several miles to Camp Ross were on dusty dirt roads. I noticed that homes and shops in several villages we drove through had a coating of dust on their tile and thatched roofs.

At the entrance to Camp Ross, we were halted at the front gate by two MPs who wanted to make sure I was who I said I was. Gary told them I was the new guy for the security team, but they still insisted on seeing my orders.

They barely glanced at my papers, handed them back to me, and told me to report to the commanding officer. Gary glared at them as we drove in and whispered to me, "that was where everyone new has to report to. These guys really didn't have to see your orders, they just want to act important."

Gary parked in front of the post commander's office, dropped me off, and said that he'd see me around. I walked into the office and met up with another spec 4, the company clerk, sitting behind a large L-shaped desk with papers stacked and skattered in front of him and a large Royal manual typewriter that he was typing on. Like Gary, he was thin and wearing very starched and pleated fatigues. I took off my hat and tucked it under my left arm.

He turned to me, and I told him my name and that I was reporting for duty. He didn't stand but reached across his desk to shake my hand and introduced himself as Mike. He had a thick Southern accent.

He told me to wait a second as he got up and knocked on the door behind him. A voice said to come in. Mike went in and told the commanding officer I was here to report for duty. Mike came back out and waved me in.

The commanding officer was a young captain, probably only a year or two older than me, and sat straight and stiff- backed at his fancy wooden desk. I walked up close to the desk, snapped to attention, saluted, and officially announced that I was reporting for duty. He returned my salute and asked for a copy of my orders.

The captain's desk was very clean and shiny. Whereas Mike the company clerk's desk was littered with papers, the captain had nothing on his desk except my orders and his brass name plate: Capt. Donald Chapman.

Captain Chapman initiated a little small talk, asking me where I came from, and what did I plan to do when I got out. He also had a Southern accent, and said he was from Atlanta. He appeared to be a little stocky, but in a muscular way.

Finally, he called Mike in and told him to take me to get me settled in my new home and that tomorrow I would meet the officers and NCOs I'd be working with.

I was led to a small building that was barracks for a half dozen soldiers. Mike showed me my bed, which had the mattress rolled up, but with clean sheets and pillow on top of it, all ready for me. Next to the bed were two metal lockers where I would be hanging my clothes. The shelves, inside near the top, were where I would keep my shaving and bathroom gear.

Mike hung around talking to me while I was unloading my duffel and laundry bags. He told me it was close to quitting time, and my five bunk mates would be coming in soon. He wanted to introduce me to them.

Barely fifteen minutes later, they started filtering in. The first to come in was Korean, a Sergeant Kim, who I found out when introduced, was a KATUSA. I asked him what a KATUSA was. He spoke English quite well and with hardly an accent.

"It stands for Korean Augmentation To the USA. We KATUSAs are part of the Republic of Korea Army, known as ROKA, but are attached to the US Army. Nearly all of us live in

Army bases and have military occupations like you American soldiers. We do a lot of translating from Korean to English and sometimes the other way around when doing combined field training with the ROKAs."

He went on to tell me that every Korean man is drafted and must serve in the military for 21 months. To be a KATUSA, each must get a high English test score. Almost all of them were college students and highly educated.

I found out later that KATUSAs made hardly any money and relied on the free base services, like mess hall food and the service club.

When he finished telling me all this, three more guys came in. All three were corporals. Mike introduced Cliff, a brown-haired, short guy (around 5'8") from Seattle, a blond guy called Gumby, real name Todd, around 6'2", thin and gangly, from Des Moines, and Roland, who went by Butch, another brown-haired guy, my height, who came from Queens. All but Butch seemed nice and shook my hand vigorously. Butch just waved and said "hey" and sat down on his bunk.

A few minutes later, one more arrived, a Buck Sergeant. The name Buck Sergeant is not an official army name. It denotes the first stage of being a sergeant. Three chevron bars on the sleeves. He had slightly dark skin and looked Latino. His black hair was a little longer than all the rest of us and appeared slicked back. He also sported a pencil-thin mustache. Mike introduced him as Carlos, a Puerto Rican from Brooklyn.

Carlos came over to me, looked me up and down without smiling, then grabbed my hand with both of his and said, "Welcome to the asshole of Korea!"

Cliff and Gumby laughed and told Carlos to take it easy on the new guy. Carlos also laughed and kept shaking my hand.

"No, really, welcome Ron."

Everyone then headed to the latrine to wash up for an evening out, which I later understood happened nightly. Mike had to leave but told me one more guy might or might not show up. He said the last guy's name was Curtis and was a Black Buck Sergeant from New Orleans. He didn't show up. I later found out he'd been in the army for nearly 20 years and had been demoted for some reason from Sergeant First Class to Sergeant. Buck Sergeant.

It was almost 9pm when I finished putting all my clothes away and arranging everything in the Army way. I did all my ablutions in the latrine, which was a room through a door in the back of the barracks, stripped down to my underwear, and crawled into bed with one of the books I brought along. By 2200 hours (10pm) I was asleep.

That first night at Camp Ross was too short. The nighttime CQ (Charge of Quarters) came through waking everyone up at 5:30am. I started to make my bed, and Gumby said not to. A Korean houseboy comes at six to make beds, clean the barracks, and do our laundry. Everyone paid him five dollars a month each to take care of the place.

I had a half hour to do the three S's, get dressed, and then head to the mess hall for breakfast. Cliff and Gumby said they'd go with me, so I'd know where to go. Cliff also said he was tasked to take me to meet my three bosses at 7:30.

After breakfast I went back to the barracks to brush my teeth and get ready for my first day at work. As I walked in, the Black Buck Sergeant that had spent the night elsewhere, was sitting on his bunk across from mine. He looked bleary eyed and hung over.

Curtis looked up and smiled. I went over to him and introduced myself. He said hello in a friendly Louisiana Creole accent. He also looked much older than the rest of us in the barracks. He was a little overweight, and, when he stood up, a little shorter than me. He even had some grey hair. A salt and pepper look. Curtis told me he worked in the motor pool, and that I'd probably be driving one of the deuce-and-a-half trucks he worked on for the monthly "fact-finding" outings my bosses go on. I didn't like the sound of that.

As I went in to brush my teeth, I came face to face with the houseboy. Actually, his face came to my chest. I had to look down to see him. He was barely five feet tall, very thin, and old. I thought, not a houseboy, but a housegrandpa. He wore what looked like old olive-drab Korean army fatigues that looked a little too large for him.

I said hello. He said herro and introduced himself as Mr. Kim. Little did I know at the time that around 40% of Koreans had Kim as a last name.

It was nearly 7:30 when Cliff returned and motioned for me to follow him. I put on my hat, checked to make sure my summer uniform was all buttoned up and well-pressed and followed him outside and up the street about fifty yards. We then walked into a fairly new building with two large rooms, one in front of the other, each with a separate office for the higher-ranking officers.

I was led through a door with "S1 Office" painted on it, and into the back room. There were three desks. A very young second lieutenant sat at one, and an elderly looking master sergeant, who looked up at me with a scowl, sat at another. The third desk was empty, and I figured it would be mine.

I walked up and saluted the lieutenant and introduced myself. I had another copy of my orders and began to hand them to him. He told me that I was to give them to Captain Copeland, the commanding officer who was in his office behind a closed door. The lieutenant got up and knocked on the door. I heard a chair squeak, then the door opened to another young officer. The lieutenant looked my age. The captain couldn't have been much older.

I again saluted.

He returned the salute, and asked me to come in. He sat back down on his squeaky, leather office chair behind a highly polished mahogany desk. His brown hair was long enough to comb, at least at the top. His "sidewalls" were so short as to be almost non-existent. He was the same height as me, and seemed friendly, but I could see in his eyes, as he stared at me, that he could be stern. He had an open bible on his desk. The rest of his desk was clean, no papers, and the only thing besides the bible was his brass name plate: Capt. Raymond Copeland.

I stood at attention in front of him, said I was reporting for duty, and handed him my orders. He took a quick look at them, told me to relax and sit down, and began to tell me what his office does, and what I'd be doing.

"Camp Ross is a security compound," he began. "Our S1 office is the nerve center of the Second Division. We process all intel sent to us from operatives on both sides of the DMZ. Since you already have a classified clearance, you will be typing up some of our reports right away. When you get your secret clearance, after a thorough background check, you'll have much more work to do. In a month or so, we'll see about getting you a top-secret clearance. Any questions?"

"Sir, one of the guys told me we would be in the field occasionally. Is that true?" I asked.

"Yes. Once every month we head up to the DMZ to do our own observations of enemy activity."

"Enemies, sir?"

"There never was a truce signed. Only an armistice ending the Korean conflict fourteen years ago. We are still officially at war with North Korea. Just yesterday we got a report of sniper shots east of the Peace Center at Panmunjom. Oh, and by the way, you'll be driving our Jeep occasionally whenever one of us needs to travel somewhere, and when we go on maneuvers, you'll drive our deuce-and-a-half. You'll soon know your way around the area."

I was thinking that I'd rather just spend my tour of duty typing away at a warm, comfortable desk like what I had in

Oklahoma. Instead I got sent to a "secure" compound where all the "hush-hush" secret military info from and about North Korea was stored, maintained, and distributed to the proper authorities (CIA, CID, and other secret service types as well as government bigwigs, like our President). So now here I am in the main S1 office as a clerk and secretary to the officers and non-com who organize all the spying and prying into North Korea.

"If you have no other questions, let me take you to meet the rest of the team."

I followed him into the main office. He first introduced me to Lieutenant Bridgestone who I talked to when I came in. The lieutenant looked like he was shorter than me and very Aryan with short blond hair. He looked very young. He smiled, showing a set of perfect teeth behind thin lips.

I saluted again. He returned the salute, got up, and reached out to shake my hand. His hand was a little sweaty.

As he welcomed me to the team, I noticed the papers, pencils, and accessories on his desk were arranged in perfect order. I imagined everything was standing at attention for him.

The captain continued the introductions and took me to meet Sergeant Major Willis. He didn't stand. He didn't shake my hand. He only said, in a raspy voice, not to me, but to the lieutenant, "I'll need a driver Saturday," as he stuffed a cigarette out in an already full ashtray.

He looked short behind his big desk, and the wrinkles on his face showed he was not a young man. I took an instant dislike to him.

His metal desk was arranged just the opposite of Lieutenant Bridgestone's. I should say disarranged. Papers were scattered and piled all around him and several pencils, some broken, littered the blotter in front of him.

Captain Copeland took me to the empty desk and told me that was where I'd be working. It was an L-shaped desk with a lift-up typing area on the side L, which was up. The typewriter was a standard-size manual Royal typewriter that looked like it had been around since the 1950s. It was nearly identical to the ones I learned on in high school.

The captain then showed me where all the supplies were that I would need for my work and told me to grab a ream of paper and a package of carbon paper and have them handy in the drawer by my typewriter.

"We'll get you started today on some non-secretive transcriptions," the captain said, glancing over to the Sergeant Major. "Willis? Do you have the meeting program notes finished?"

The raspy-voiced Sergeant major didn't get up. He coughed, I figured from smoking, and said, "Yep", not yes sir, and held up several sheets of hand-written notes to the captain, making the captain come over to take them.

I was told to type in triplicate. Three sheets of paper with carbon paper between each of them.

That was the way it was for the next three weeks. A week after starting, I got my secret clearance and began typing more important notes and reports. I began driving the officers and Sergeant Major around to watch war games in an open army Jeep.

I also found that the small movie theater needed a projectionist, because the last one was leaving for home. I had used 16mm projectors before in high school and college, so it was very easy to get started. I claimed the job. The small base theater was in the dining area of the mess hall and could only be open two nights a week, Friday and Saturday.

Around the end of week three, things began to change.

I got to be good friends with Gumby. He said a variety show, put on by an Army Entertainment Corps, was performing at the service club Saturday afternoon. He knew a couple of the performers.

The show was incredibly good, and very professional. There was a backup band playing current music for several vocalists. There were Black singing groups doing Otis Redding, Sam and Dave, and Smoky Robinson type songs. They did a great job replicating those acts. There were white singing groups doing Beach Boys and Three Dog Night type songs. Again, quite good.

After the show was over, Gumby took me over to introduce me to his friends. As we talked, I told them I had been a folk singer and performed a little at college. They told me there was a position opening since someone was leaving, and I should come in for an audition next Saturday morning. I thought, "Groovy".

On Monday morning, the start of week four, I asked Captain Copeland if it would be ok for me to audition.

"Absolutely not!" the captain screamed at me. "We just got you, and you're staying here. I don't want to train someone else already!"

I was devastated, and angry.

Of course, Lieutenant Bridgestone and Sergeant Major Willis overheard that exchange. Willis smiled for the first time since I'd been there. Not a pleasant smile. Work was rather strained that day.

Feeling rebellious, when Saturday rolled around again, I was on a bus heading for Recreation Compound #1 with Gumby. It was a very fancily decorated Korean bus that smelled of rice-wine-smelling sweat. We disembarked at the front gate to RC #1.

Gumby had been to RC #1 several times and knew where his friends' barracks were. We went in and met up with them. We all then went across the compound to their rehearsal and performance hall, which was a new concrete block building with a stage on one end and an office, storage area, and bathroom in the back.

The first thing I heard was lovely classical music being played on a fairly new upright piano. I was introduced to Jeffery, whose blond hair was a little longer than the army way and parted in the middle. He seemed effeminate. He would be auditioning me.

A couple more of the entertainers arrived and stood around the piano, watching.

The audition consisted of Jeffery playing three to five notes in random patterns, and I was to sing them back in the same pattern. I aced it.

Jeffery told me that I would be hearing from their commanding officer in a few days.

On Monday I was back in the office typing away. On Tuesday morning, the Captain called me into his office. He was livid.

"You disobeyed me! You auditioned! You've been accepted! These damn orders are signed by our commanding General Thomas, so I can't rescind them. However, I can hold you up for ten days while we get a new clerk. I'm going to make the rest of your time here hell!" He screamed. He pounded his fist on his desk and made his bible bounce.

And he, and especially the Sergeant Major, did make my life hell.

Three times in ten days I had 24-hour duties. Twelve hours working in the office, and twelve hours on CQ (Charge of Quarters), doing other people's work all night.

And on one of those days on a Friday afternoon, Willis ordered me to check out a Jeep and pick him up in front of his room at the NCO quarters. I had no idea what he had in mind…

Chapter 6
The Yobo

Many, many years ago, I don't know when, since my knowledge of Oriental history is minimal, Mongol hordes overran Asia. Those invaders, to the civilized Koreans, were ugly and uncultured Barbarians. Centuries later, Japanese hordes overran China and Korea. Again, they were seen as Barbarians. After World War II, Korea was officially split into North and South. North Korea had the backing of Soviet and Chinese Communists, and in 1950 they rushed south in an attempt to unify Korea as a single Communist country. The United Nations forces rushed north to push the Red Menace back to where they came from. This was the start of the Korean War. Always in the eyes of the Koreans caught in the middle, those coming from either direction were all uncultured Barbarians.

The Korean Conflict ended with an armistice, the country was divided, and U.S. troops remain in the South to this day. They were still considered Barbarians, and "ugly Americans," as Eugene Burdick and William Lederer very pointedly wrote in their novel in 1958.

I didn't think of myself as a Barbarian when I first arrived in Korea in 1967. Barbarians were supposed to look like Yul Brynner and ride into villages on horseback swinging swords and carrying off beautiful women. Me, a Barbarian? No, I was a young American barely two years past being a teenager having no knowledge of how other cultures lived. I only knew that I didn't want to be there. I was drafted, and only by chance, or blind luck, was sent to Korea instead of Vietnam. Even though I found out shortly after I arrived that Korea was still considered, unofficially, a war zone, I had no idea why we were still guarding the border for little Oriental men and women who pissed on the roadsides. That, to me, was Barbarian.

As an S1 clerk at Camp Ross, I had the duty to drive my superiors around in an open Jeep. I also had to drive everyone else in the office anywhere they wanted to go. The captain and head of these officers and non-coms was a 24-year-old, who, in one breath, told you how good a Christian he was, then, in another breath, tried to court-martial you for having a button missing on your uniform. He's the one who tried to court martial me for auditioning for the General's Chorus but was only able to give me an Article 15, non-judicial punishment, the Kangaroo Court, which kept me there working hard for ten days before I could transfer.

Second in command was a 20-year-old second lieutenant with no apparent knowledge beyond what he learned in Officer Candidate School (in other words, he knew nothing of life and less of people). I usually only drove him to the PX in another Army camp down the road.

Third in command (but ready to tell you he was the real boss of the outfit), was the Sergeant Major. He claimed to be a better Christian, a better soldier, and a better man than anyone in all of God's army, and he always put himself above the heathen gooks, as he called them, who we were supposed to be protecting. He looked around sixty years old to me, probably because he chain smoked, but was really in his forties. He continually boasted of his sexual prowess, even with his "disability." Over and over again he told me he lost a testicle during the Korean War and bragged that he had more sexual stamina than any man with a full set; he said he could still father an army. And I know he tried.

During that ten-day Kangaroo Court assignment at Camp Ross, I saw the ugly Americans Burdick and Lederer described. Career soldiers like the Sergeant Major, wanted to be waited on and served by everyone. They acted holier than thou and showed no concern for the people we were sworn to protect. No, it didn't take very long to notice that the Koreans never saw us at our best. And it was always the soldiers who were most visible roaming the streets, trespassing on and defiling properties, stealing roadside shrines and artifacts to take home as souvenirs, appearing intoxicated most of the time; and bargaining for and buying young Korean girls, from around 12 years old on up, to use as Yobos.

Now, "Yobo" has several meanings. The least degrading definition is a Korean woman who is a soldier's steady girlfriend. Over the years many soldiers became infatuated with and married Korean women.   However, to Koreans, interracial couplings were forbidden and a daughter who married outside her race was disowned by her family.

Another definition of Yobo is a Korean prostitute visited by a soldier on a regular basis. Thousands of poor, young girls found out they could make a good living servicing soldiers, and girls who were able to retain regular customers lived better than most.

The worst definition of Yobo, and one that was all too common, is a Korean girl bought from her parents or guardian by a soldier to be used as a concubine, or, more accurately, a sex slave.

A Yobo is the product of two completely different cultures clashing. It is a form of prostitution that never would have come about without the help of the American GI. Of course, there have always been prostitutes around army bases, and in Korea long before we arrived, but since the end of the Korean Conflict our soldiers created situations where they could buy a girl to keep during their tour of duty. There were a few who bought several and set up their own harems and some who became pimps.

The "sort-of" etymology of the word, Yobo, was rumored to have begun during the Korean Conflict with the prostitutes yelling out to passing soldiers, "yoboseo," which means no more than "hello" in Korean. This greeting would be followed by lewd Pidgin English come-ons. The soldiers quickly picked up on this greeting and almost immediately begin echoing it back to the prostitutes, and more often to any young girl they passed. Of course, GIs associated this common greeting with prostitutes and soon shortened it to Yobo.

When I first arrived in Korea, besides that painful gamma globulin shot, I also had to go through an orientation lecture. One of the first comments was that venturing from the safety of a compound was extremely dangerous, especially in the area north of Seoul, where I would be stationed. My own nervous tension that one month at Camp Ross I blamed on the deadly tension I was told pervaded the countryside. What I wasn't told, however, was that the two Koreas were again on the verge of war. The S1 office where I worked constantly reported increased enemy activities along the DMZ, and even over the border into South Korea. Rumors abounded that Commies and Commie sympathizers were all over the place, and we should all stay on base and out of the villages.

This threat didn't keep most of the soldiers I now lived with cooped up. Some in our barracks raced to the village every night right after work. Some jumped on Army shuttles, Korean buses, or taxis. If they had enough stripes or brass, they checked out a Jeep from the motor pool and headed several miles north to the "turkey farm" for a quickie with one of the girls. And those in the speeding Jeeps took over the roads, often forcing the native pedestrians and bicyclists off the road into rice paddies. And some of the soldiers, those with enough rank to afford it, went home to their yobos.

At the end of work one Friday, during the time of my ten-day article 15 (Kangaroo Court) duties, the Sergeant Major was anxious, so to speak, and decided he needed a little recreation. He asked me to check out the company jeep and meet him in front of his hootch, the NCO quarters where he lived, right after dinner at 6:30.

This same old guy had put every soldier north of Seoul on high alert that morning on the rumor that North Korean infiltrators were being hidden by villagers in the area. Threat of war didn't stop the Sergeant Major from getting a little nookie.

I drove him out of the compound, and he directed me a quarter mile north along a pitted and ridged one-lane dirt road that wound about the edges of the rice paddies between Seoul and Panmunjom. He told me to hurry, and the cloud of dust that followed us coated and choked everyone we passed.

After a quick, bone-jarring ride, we drove down a short side road—more like a cow path—and pulled up in front of a small, single-story, thatch-roofed farmhouse that was on the edge of the road. It appeared to be made of mud and had a rice-stalk thatched roof covered with a thick layer of dust. The front and sides were freshly whitewashed and clean. This was the home of the Sergeant Major's yobo.

His yobo, he told me on the drive over, was half American. Her father was a soldier who had passed through the area in 1953, and her mother now lived in Pusan with a Naval officer. The Sergeant Major bought the girl six months ago from her guardian, a mama-san who ran a bar and brothel just outside our compound gate. Some quick adding in my head made me painfully realize his yobo couldn't be more than thirteen. He told me she now lived with her grandmother.

After pulling up in front of the house, the Sergeant Major leapt out of the jeep like a playful colt, trotting around the car with his head high and, it seemed, nostrils flaring. I swear he whinnied. He brushed past a toothless old woman, the grandmother, I figured, who was squatting next to the front door. He didn't bother to glance her way, offer her a greeting, or apologize for nearly running her over. The woman looked at him as he ran by, frowned, squinted her permanently squinted eyes even more, said something low and guttural, and spit on the ground where he had passed. She then looked at me and stared. And stared.

The Sergeant Major was in such a hurry to leave the compound that I forgot to bring anything to read, so I tried to pass the time by catnapping in the warm setting sun. Unfortunately, I was parked facing the old woman, and every time I opened my eyes, I saw her staring at me. Once when I opened my eyes, I thought I saw someone else looking at me from one of the windows. He was in the shadows, but I was sure he was a Korean soldier. Which Korea, I couldn't tell. I felt myself shaking, not from cold, but fright.

The face in the window disappeared. And the old woman kept staring at me. Her eyes never left me. I felt the heat of her tiny slits radiating anger, which I imagined must have built up over the years. Her face, leathery and furrowed like elephant skin, seemed to grow more menacing as the minutes slowly ticked by. There I sat, a lowly unarmed private, imagining that she, squatting next to a sharp, wooden pitchfork and a hand scythe, could be my executioner at any moment. She could be a North Korean sympathizer. The guy I saw in the window could be pointing a gun at me. She could have a cache of hand grenades hidden under her peasant dress. No, I didn't like being in an open jeep this close to her and the hut.

I tried to gather my courage and to smile at her and nodded a greeting. Her expression didn't change. At almost the same time the sudden sound of a young girl's shrill laughter and the old Sergeant Major's strained moaning broke the silence. In a few seconds his moans became more frequent until a very audible gasp signaled his climax. I closed my eyes, leaned forward, and bumped my head a few times on the steering wheel in embarrassment. I glanced at the old woman. She still stared. Her face was still frozen in a slant-eyed scowl. Her hand was on the pitchfork. I wanted to speed away and leave the old Sergeant Major to deal with the woman and whoever it was I saw at the window. Also, I was so embarrassed I didn't want to face him again after hearing such an intimate act exhibited so openly. And I didn't want to stay there facing the old woman anymore. She probably thought I was no better than the Sergeant. After all, I was in the U.S. Army. Barbarian.

More feminine giggling and masculine exclamations invaded my ears as I twitched in the car seat trying to avoid what seemed like the increasingly hostile gaze of the woman. I was sure she was giving me the evil eye and trying to plant some sinister Oriental curse on me.

A half-hour later, with the Autumn sun setting behind the barren hills, a grinning and much more slowly moving Sergeant Major walked out the door nodding to someone inside as he left. His eyes had the droopy appearance of a sleepy, over-sated jackal that had just devoured a large piece of carrion.

As much as I despised him for putting me through such discomfort, I was glad to see him slide into the seat beside me. There's safety in numbers, I felt, and the old woman, and whoever else was there, wouldn't dare do anything to me now.

I started the engine almost before the Sergeant Major sat down, put the jeep in gear, made a quick U-turn, and headed back towards camp, leaving the old woman in a cloud of dust. In the rearview mirror I could just make out the old woman getting up and walking over to where the jeep had been. With her pitchfork in her hand, she spat at us and violently poked her pitchfork in the ground. A young Korean man in an unfamiliar uniform came out and stood beside her looking at us. I shivered.

The Sergeant Major was very satisfied with himself, and his ego was erect to a point of bursting, which it did with a flow of descriptive comments about every intimate detail of his encounter. He told me about his affair, twice, on the way back, leaving nothing out. My stomach hurt from disgust and my head hurt from the constant bragging.

Later that evening I thought about that young Korean girl the Sergeant Major bought and what she would do when he left for the States, which was to happen a few weeks after that incident. I thought about the old woman sitting outside the house. I thought about the face at the window. The Sergeant Major said grandma was an old widow. She took care of the house and the grounds so his yobo would have nothing to do but take care of him. She was part of his yobo purchase deal.

I wanted to spend the remaining few hours in my bunk with my journal, before I had to go back on duty, putting down all I could remember about that day. I had just begun to write when one of my "buddies" came up to me and asked if I wanted to go with him to visit his yobo...who has a sister, ...that can use some money, ...that will do anything. Her mama-san will bargain, you could get her cheap...

He wondered why I put my pillow over my face and screamed into it.

Finally, my ten days of detention were over. I had all my stuff packed, said goodbye to the only two in the barracks I'd become friends with, hopped on a small, dented Korean taxi smelling of cigarettes, mokkoli (Korean rice wine), and sweat, rode about five miles down another dusty road, and got dropped off at the gate of Recreation Compound #1.

I was nervous about starting out my new version of army life and didn't know what to expect. I did know, however, that playing music and singing was going to be a whole lot better than where I had been at Camp Ross.

I schlepped my bags to the base office, walked in and met up with Darren, the company clerk. He looked my age, but with blond hair and a thin blond mustache. He cheerfully welcomed me, and then lifted the phone to announce my arrival to the base commander, Lieutenant Bowman. I was to go in and report to him.

I left my bags with Darren, who got up and opened the door for me, and I walked in to meet up with a good looking young Black lieutenant. He also sported a thin mustache.

I stood at attention, saluted, and announced I was reporting for duty. He returned my salute, then got up and reached out to shake my hand. He was taller than me by at least two inches and seemed to have an athletic build.

"Welcome to the General's Chorus, Ron," Lieutenant Bowman said. He went on to tell me, "You will be singing with the chorus once a month at the commanding general's mess. This is a big dinner for around two to three dozen of the big brass here in second division and I-corps. Our general loves martial music rousingly sung by all of you, and he is the one who set up this full-time entertainment corps last year. You will also be part of the touring variety show or be in one of the touring rock or blues groups. I think the current opening for you is in the variety show."

I asked a few questions about the compound, then Lieutenant Bowman called in Darren to take me to the hootch, my new home.

We walked the short distance to the hootch, and Darren pointed out some of the amenities at RC#1.

"And over there is the bowling alley," he said as he turned and pointed behind us. "It's eight alleys and very busy on the weekends. If you like to bowl, weekdays are best. It's nearly empty. Next to the bowling alley are the clubs. Officer's club on the right, NCOs' club in the middle, and the servicemen's club on the left. Cheap drinks and slot machines. Across from those is the Service Club, run by the donut dollies."

"Uh, donut dollies?" I asked.

"Red Cross ladies. There's three of them here. They serve coffee and donuts and talk to lonely servicemen. The head lady, Valerie, is the lieutenant's current girlfriend. She pretty much runs the place. Some of the groups play there once in a while. I think James Brown is coming in a month or two on a USO tour."

"Wow. That'll be groovy."

"You'll find out more about this compound while you're here. There's a good-sized PX where you can get the latest records, as well as goodies to eat. There's also a kind of burger bar and soda fountain in there. Not bad burgers. There's also a photo lab that sells cameras and film. Over there," Darren pointed to a quonset hut building, "is a wood shop. The Korean in there can make anything out of wood, and you can work on stuff yourself.

"The rest of the compound has a football field, baseball field, and a basketball court for those who are sports inclined. Ah... here we are."

Darren led me into a U-shaped metal building with a metal roof. The number on the outside said T-30. I asked Darren what that meant.

"The T stands for temporary. These are buildings left over from the occupation after the Korean war. They were supposed to be removed at some point but never were. There's no insulation, so they're hot in the summer and freezing in the winter. There're space heaters, but they only warm the area a few feet around them."

When I saw my assigned bed, lockers (two), and kimchi stand (a bedside table), I began to wonder what I had gotten myself into.

The bed was an old-style bunk bed, but without a bunk on top. It was narrow, and the mattress looked only a few inches thick. A pile of folded olive drab blankets and a set of sheets were stacked on the small, thin pillow. My bed was far from a space heater at the end of one of the U's and by one of the doors.

I dropped my bags on the bed, and Darren excused himself saying that I'd shortly get to know everyone, as they'd be in from rehearsal soon.

As I began to empty my bags some of my new hootch mates began to drift in. Each one introduced himself as they walked by to their own areas.

"Hi. I'm Tom," the first one said. I introduced myself. "But you can call me Booser." He was a short, slim white guy in wrinkled fatigue shirt and pants. His thin lips were constantly smiling, and his blue eyes sparkled. He shook my hand, then excused himself and trotted to the other end of the building to his own bunk.

The next ones passing by were a pair of Black guys, almost identical in appearance. Both were in very pressed and pleated fatigue uniforms, and both were the same height and slim, but wiry and physically fit. I introduced myself to them.

"Hey Ron," they both said together. Then separately, one said, "I'm Toby. He's Tyler. We all do the Sam and Dave act for the variety show. Good to see you here."

The other said to me, "Yeah. Welcome to the asshole of Korea."

I had heard that before. So, I took a few seconds to take that in, then said, quietly, but Toby caught what I said, "I thought it was the latrine of Korea."

Toby laughed and stayed with me, and Tyler left in what looked like an angry huff.

"Don't mind him. He's had a hard life in the South that white guys made harder for him. You seem ok. You do boo?"

"Uh… boo?" I questioned.

"Pot. Maryjane. Weed."

"A little," I replied. "I went to college."

"It's like a religion here. Once you get set in…"

He didn't get to finish, when the choral master walked in, Toby reached over and shook my hand and headed off to his own area.

It was Jeffery, who had auditioned me at the piano when I first came here to RC#1.

"Welcome to the General's Chorus," he said, not really looking at me, but past me, in kind of an officious tone."

Tomorrow, you'll go to the rehearsal hall to meet everyone else in our group. You'll also be in the variety show. We'll have to hook you up with someone you can sing with. Besides the chorus, you must not only entertain troops, but do Korean goodwill shows, and sometimes play on Armed Forces Radio. We tour every two months for up to two weeks from Panmunjom to Pusan."

"Wow." I said, then thought I should ingratiate myself to him. "I really look forward to that."

With that, Jeffery did a limp wrist wave and walked quickly away.

I finally emptied my bags and arranged them in my locker. I put the book I was reading on the kimchi stand next to my bunk. A small non-opening window was between my bunk and the next one. I didn't see any overhead lighting, and noticed the other bunks had table lamps. In walked a tall stocky guy with a bush of curly red hair and an almost bushy red mustache. The name on the left side of his fatigue shirt said Mosher. What was different about his shirt was that the U.S. Army tag on the right side said Le Armée Suisse.

"Howdy," he said with absolutely no accent as he sat down on my bunk. "I'm Chuck Mosher. And you?"

I told him, and then asked, "Where are you from, and what is Le Armée Suisse?"

"California. Los Altos. In the San Francisco Bay area. My Swiss Army tag is just to screw with Top, our paranoid sergeant."

"Los Altos, huh? I'm from Sunnyvale originally. …uh, what do you mean paranoid?"

"It's rumored our sergeant lost most of his men in Vietnam through incompetence and the survivors have sworn to kill him for it. He's the only NCO… actually, the only anyone on base with a gun. He's constantly got his loaded 45 strapped to his waist."

"Jesus. I hope I don't have to deal with him while I'm here."

"He's afraid of most of us and stays away most of the time."

"Do we ever have to do stupid Army stuff here?"

"We haven't since I've been here. We do have to dress up in fancy uniforms for the big brass dinner once a month, though. I have to head to the latrine. See you around."

"I'll be here."

No one else popped by for a while, so I was able to finish getting my area ready.

I noticed the bunk next to me was vacant too, and since it had a lamp, I snuck over, unplugged it, and brought it back to my kimchi stand, so now I'd be able to read at night.

By the time I finished setting up my area, it was nearly 4pm. I had missed lunch and was pretty hungry, so I headed over to the PX soda fountain. It was a very basic setting with a counter and backless Naugahyde upholstered stools. The menu was just as basic: hamburgers, grilled cheese, a few sandwiches (all on white bread), sodas, and milk shakes. I sat down and ordered a cheeseburger and Coke from the short, cute Korean girl behind the counter. Her name tag said Miss Kim.

She was not only the waitress, but the cook and washer. She jumped from one customer to another to the grill to the sink and back again. I was intrigued with her efficiency… and how cute she was. It had now been over a month since I'd seen my girlfriend, and I kept staring, semi-lustfully, at Miss Kim.

When she returned with my burger and drink, I was the only one left at the counter, so I asked her a simple question to break the ice. "Do you speak English?"

She replied, "Yes, I do," in near-perfectly accented English. "I learned in Seoul High School. English was a requirement."

Seems almost perfect to me. Like Orientals learning English, Ls and Rs are a little difficult since they are not in, or very seldom in, their languages. She did slur over her Ls and Rs, but she spoke English very well.

"Do you work here all the time?" I asked.

"I work five days, Monday through Friday. Miss Kim works Saturday and Sunday."

"Another Miss Kim?"

"It is a common name in Korea. It is my married name."

Married. Damn.

She rushed off to do more dish washing.

I finished my burger, which wasn't bad, then went back to my hootch.

When I got to my bunk, there were three Black guys standing in the area in front of me smoking and laughing and talking in what sounded to me like Black street lingo. I waved at them, and one came over to introduce himself.

"Hi new guy. I'm Tom Johnson, but everyone calls me T.J."

I introduced myself.

54

"Those two are Porter and Art." Porter waved; Art looked the other way. Another Black who didn't seem to like white guys, I figured. "We sing together in the show as The Expressions. You know, doo wop and soul like Little Anthony and the Imperials and the Temptations."

"That sounds cool. I look forward to being in the show."

"It is fun, but hard work. We rehearse every morning 'til noon, Monday through Friday for the General's Chorus, then rehearse until dinner on our music and acts. Friday night and sometimes all day Saturday and Sunday we travel to other service clubs to perform. Sometimes we do two shows a day afternoon and evening."

"Jeez, T.J., that does sound like work. Good thing I like to sing."

T.J. shook my hand. Porter came over and did the same. Art didn't. The three of them headed further into the building.

I was pretty tired and was thinking about getting into bed and reading a little, when I was confronted by two more guys, both white.

"Hey, new guy, "the first one said. "I'm Billy."

The other said, "Hi. I'm Mike. We do a singing act. We used to be a trio, but the other guy turned out and went home. You want to join up?"

I introduced myself and shook hands with them as I replied. "Sure. I heard you were the act I was to probably going to get into."

"That's great," said both Billy and Mike. Billy continued, "Once you get settled in, we can talk about where to go from here. We'll need two songs to do for the show that starts in two weeks."

I said that if they had time, we could talk about it now and get to know each other better. They both sat down at the end of my bunk, one on each side.

Billy was from Des Moines and was shorter than me by a couple of inches. He was stocky, but not overweight, and had a chubby, kind of baby face, clean shaven and with slightly long brunette hair parted and slicked down. As the conversation continued, I found out he had been a singer in a symphony chorus but liked doing current pop tunes.

Mike was a dark-haired Italian from Queens and grew up singing in a Catholic church choir. He kind of reminded me of Dean Martin. He was my height and looked as thin as me. His black hair was as long as Billy's, parted and slicked down the same way.

Both of them were originally stationed across the road at Camp Casey, the Second Division armor headquarters. When they went across the street to RC1, they found out about the Entertainment Corps and auditioned, like I did, and were transferred almost immediately.

We talked for nearly an hour but didn't get into what songs to do. They then headed off to the PX for burgers. I was tired from my last ten days of kangaroo court and the transfer and didn't want to go out again. I went next door to the latrine and did my tooth and body duties, but as soon as my head hit the pillow, nothing could wake me up.

I awoke at six in the morning, like I was used to at the security compound. The hootch was quiet except for the sound of snores echoing through the building.

I wrapped my bath towel around my waist, grabbed my soap, shampoo, and shaving gear and went over to the latrine to do my three S's.

The latrine was one of the newer buildings and made of concrete blocks. It was approximately 40 feet square. There were two entrances, one on each side of the middle room where all the sinks and mirrors were. There were twelve sinks, six on each side of the room. Two rooms came off the sink room. One had a dozen toilets, six lining each wall, and the other was the shower room.

One S down, I walked into the shower room. It was around fifteen feet square with twelve showerheads, four on three walls. I was the only one in there.

The water was nice and warm, at least until someone came in and flushed a toilet. I did a short dance as the water went from hot, to cool, then back to warm.

Two S's down. With my towel wrapped around me, I commandeered a sink, lathered up, and did my final S.

By the time I traipsed back to my bunk, other guys were up and moving around. I got dressed and made my way to the mess hall for breakfast. Here, they actually asked me how I wanted my eggs and cooked them to order. Usually, on army bases, you get whatever is in the steam table containers. I felt like I was at a diner.

While eating, I was joined by Billy and Mike. At nine, we were to go rehearse the General's Chorus. After lunch, we were to start working on our new act together.

A little before nine I walked the hundred yards to the rehearsal hall with Billy and Mike. The large concrete block building looked almost new. It was two stories high, but inside, it was a high-ceilinged auditorium. A good-sized stage ran along one end, with a small dressing room on one side and stage light panels on the other. In the back was a storage room and an office. The open floor was concrete with beige linoleum tiles. Tiered platforms were set up in front of the stage. This is where the General's Chorus would stand and rehearse.

Mike signaled for me to follow him, and we walked into the office. There were two desks. At one was the choir master, Jeffery, who didn't even look up from his music notes, and the other was introduced as Benny, who turned out to be the guy who booked the shows and tours and sometimes was a roadie and drove the Special Services van for the groups.

More guys arrived and milled around joking and laughing. One sat down at a new-looking upright piano and began playing some Dave Brubeck style jazz. He barely got a minute into *Take Five* when Jeffery came out of the office and yelled "Enough of that, Craig. Okay, everyone up in the stands. Hey, new guy," he yelled over to me. "uh… what's your name again? Oh yeah, Ron. We need you in the tenor section, right there." He pointed to the middle of the second row.

It probably didn't matter what section I was put in. I had a wide vocal range from bass to high tenor. Singing tenor was very comfortable for me.

I was put next to the basses, who were Toby, Porter, and a white guy I hadn't yet met. His army name tag said Greenberg. He said hi, shook my hand and leaned over to whisper to me. "I'm Ira. You need a loan, see me. You need cameras or stereos, see me. Girls? See me."

I didn't know how to reply to that and just said hi back.

There was a space in the basses, and I figured someone hadn't arrived yet.

Next to me in the tenor section were Booser, T.J., Mike, and Art. The tenor section looked the biggest and took up the whole second tier and part of the first. Billy and Tyler were also in this group. Most of the others I hadn't yet met. One, a muscular looking Hispanic, turned to me and introduced himself as Jesus Garcia, then handed me a small printed flyer. (Crud. He's a Jehovah's Witness.)

There were three on the remainder of the first tier who were supposed to be altos. Mosher had just come in and was in that group. He was the tallest at six feet. The other two, one Black, one white, both of whom I hadn't met, were at least six inches shorter than Chuck.

Chuck walked up the stand to Billy, put his arm around him, and began to dry hump his side like a puppy. Everyone, except Jeffery of course, laughed as Billy yelped and pushed Chuck away. Jeffery yelled, "Mosher! Quit screwing around and get the fuck down where you belong!"

Chuck feigned lowering his head in shame and sang in a very good operatic falsetto, "Castrati, castrati, mi castrati, làmame mis cojones."

Garcia was the only one who understood the words and told Chuck he was going to hell.

"We're already there." Chuck replied.

Several other guys were talking, laughing, and generally goofing off and upsetting Jeffery for around five minutes more until Lieutenant Bowman walked in. Everyone quieted and popped to attention.

"At ease," Bowman said as he walked up the stand to the empty space in the bass section. "Okay, Jeffery, let's get started. I've got to get back to the office in ninety minutes."

Jeffery handed a stack of song books to Chuck who took one and passed them on.

For an hour and a half, we practiced a few rousing martial and military songs like *Battle Hymn of the Republic*, *Ballad of the Green Berets*, and *Gary Owen*. Jeffery was in his element setting up the harmonies and directing the chorus.

That afternoon after lunch, Mike, Billy and I sat around Mike's bunk, picked two songs off albums to work on, listened to them a few times, and began practicing our harmonies. We decided on two current rock songs, *You've Got Your Troubles*, by the Fortunes, and *Tobacco Road*, by the Nashville Teens. We duplicated the vocals to the note.

After hearing me sing, Mike and Billy thought I should be the lead singer, with them doing the backup harmonies.

Three weeks later, after we'd perfected the two songs and had worked with the variety show band, it was time for a dress rehearsal. My first performance was coming up Friday night at our RC#1 service club. Then Saturday, it was time for the General's Mess at the officer's club in Seoul. Time for the General's Chorus to sing.

Friday evening, the service club was full. Some 300 folding chairs had been set up on the floor by the donut dollies and their Korean help. All seats were taken and another hundred or so were lined up along the walls.

At seven, the variety show band swung into their opening number. The theme for this tour was *Listen My Friends*, which was a hit song by Moby Grape. That was the opening song. Originally, Moby Grape did it with three lead guitars, bass and drums. The variety show band did it with one lead guitar, sax, trumpet and trombone, plus bass and drums. The lead guitarist, Steve, and the bass player, Jack, did the vocals.

When that song finished, and while the audience applauded and cheered, the band jumped right into a soul number as Toby and Tyler came out and did *Hold On, I'm Coming* then followed that with *Soul Man*, which got the whole audience whooping, hollering, and clapping.

Then, it was my turn.

As soon as the clapping died down, the band went into *Tobacco Road*. Mike, Billy, and I came out in matching Tom Jones/Engelbert Humperdinck wide-lapel shirts open to our belts. As the lead, I was in the middle with a thin black vest. We did it flawlessly. The crowd seemed enthusiastic, but I noticed not as excited as with the Toby and Tyler act. I also noticed that at least half the audience was Black. They wanted soul.

You've Got Your Troubles got the audience going a little more. But when T.J., Porter, and Art came out and finished *My Girl* and *Get Ready*, the whole joint jumped. Yes, the audience wanted more soul. The band did the Rascals' song *Good Lovin'*, and then the lead guitarist introduced the comedy act, Mosher and Booser.

Chuck faked an Irish accent and played an army Catholic chaplain. Booser gave confession. It was about a ten-minute act, and the band did some sound effects in the background. Surprisingly, they were well received.

The band went into a soul vamp while Chuck's and Tom's props were taken off stage. As soon as it was cleared and a mike was set up, Porter came out and did a perfect Otis Redding imitation and sang *I've Been Loving You Too Long* and *Try a Little Tenderness*.

The audience was going wild and wanted more of him as Porter left the stage, but immediately came back and jumped into *Stand by Me*.

It was time for the show to end, and when Porter finally left the stage, Chuck came out acting as MC, still in his fake army chaplain outfit, and thanked everyone for coming just as the band went back into *Listen My Friends* for one verse and closed the show.

We were all exhausted when we returned to the hootch, and several joints got passed around. Chuck came over and sat on my bunk and passed a joint to me. Up to now, I'd avoided boo, but in a moment of weakness, and tiredness, I toked. And toked. And toked.

Oh wow. Far out!

Most of us slept in. Only Jeffery and Jesus were up by six. Neither of them was in the show or in the audience. We found out later that both had gone into the village. Jesus had been trying to convert Korean prostitutes, so he said. Jeffery, I didn't know what he did in the village. He wasn't into girls, I'd heard.

After finally waking up around 9, un-stoned, Chuck, Tom and I went to the PX to get something to eat. The mess hall had already closed. Miss Kim made us pancakes.

Jeffery wanted everyone to practice a little for that night's General's Mess. Everyone moseyed to the rehearsal hall, and we practiced the four songs we were to perform.

By 5 pm, we were all dressed in our dress uniforms and boarded the army bus that would take us into Seoul.

It was only an hour's drive, mostly on dirt roads, and we had to keep the windows closed so we wouldn't get covered in road dirt. It was stuffy.

By 6:30, we were hanging out in a side room waiting for our cue. The brass were just finishing up their main course. We were to sing right after dessert.

Finally, our cue. The Second and ICorps divisions' brass were all there. Glancing through the door, there were at least thirty majors, colonels, and generals, one to four stars, seated around a U-shaped table. We took our place in front of the open U, facing the brass.

We all sang flawlessly. After our three martial music rousers, we finished up with *God Bless America*. Some of the tough brass had tears in their eyes when we finished. They all applauded, we snapped to attention, then they applauded more when the commanding general came up to us, shook Jeffery's hand and saluted us. They loved it. We were glad it was over for that month.

Sunday. A day of rest. A day of goofing off, bowling, drinking, smoking, toking, reading, drawing. Several guys had spent the night in the village with either their yobos or turkey farm prostitutes and filtered back into the compound throughout the day.

Later that afternoon, Ira returned from the village with a box of food. Several of us were already fairly stoned and the zuzus, a name we gave to snack food while high, looked good. In the box were a dozen warm and large pot-sticker-like items Ira called yakomondo. They smelled good. Ira offered them to the group of us hanging out by Chuck's bunk.

I ate one. It tasted pretty good. Spicy. Ira was grinning and began to laugh after we all had our fill. "How do you like dog?" Ira said between laughs.

"Dog?" We all said in unison.

Three guys ran outside and immediately upchucked.

I just shrugged and told Ira, "Sneaky, but it did taste good." I was too stoned to care.

Monday morning it was back to the choral grind. Jeffery told us another new guy was arriving later that day.

Chapter 8
Birds of a Feather

The day John arrived Ira was lighting his farts.

This wasn't something he did all the time, but there was a bet going on, and he knew he had a pair of suckers on his hands. Two privates from the Armor division across the street were sure Ira couldn't do it and put down a couple of ten spots as a wager. Of course, money was enough incentive for Ira to do anything, including lighting farts.

And what a show it was for John when he was escorted into the barracks by the company clerk.

John had his duffel bag slung over one shoulder and his laundry bag over the other. He was standing in the doorway.

"Hey, Ira," said Darren, the company clerk. "Come on. I'm bringing a new guy in here. What kind of impression do you want to give him, anyway?"

"Fuck you," Ira said as he dropped his pants and bent over. "Kiss this or get lost."

"Ah, go fuck yourself, asshole," Darren shot back. "Come on, John, your bunk is down here on the end. Those two wall lockers are yours as well as that footlocker and kimchi stand under the window. And that's Ron, our other new guy. He's been here a few weeks now."

"Mucho gusto," I said.

"El gusto es mio. Soy John."

"¿A donde vas ahora ...John?"

"A la clase de Español. Y usted?"

"Yo tambien."

"Bueno. Vamos a clase."

"What?" said Darren.

"¿Que? Oh. Sorry Darren. First year high-school Spanish," I answered as I shook hands with John. "It seems we both took the same Spanish course."

"Do you know each other?"

"No," John answered this time. "But we went to different schools together at the same time."

"Huh?"

Darren was lost. He had very little sense of humor, which made him the brunt of occasional jokes.

"Jesus," Darren mumbled as he was leaving. "Give 'em a few days and they'll be lighting farts, too."

As he walked by Ira's bunk, that area came alive with the mixed sounds of a fart, a flame, yells and laughter. The noise frightened Darren, and he shot an angered glance towards Ira then trotted out the door.

John and I looked at each other and smiled those half-assed smiles that mark servicemen stationed in war zones. We shook hands again and formally introduced ourselves. I sat on my bunk, right across from his, and we told each other our respective histories.

England was John's birthplace. His father had been a paratrooper stationed in England during World War II. His mother was a munitions worker in Leicester who was engaged to a British military man fighting on the continent. John's father apparently swept his mother off her feet and away from the British soldier. Then, as his father was leaving to go back to the front, his mother was left pregnant and waving goodbye from the munitions plant gate. Honest. After the war, John's father came back for her and took her back to America shortly after John was born.

Music had always been a major part of John's life. He and his best buddy, Allison, had played music together for a long time. After high school they formed a band, called The Druids, playing songs patterned after the current British hits. They also acted as if they were British with mop top haircuts and fake accents. They became slightly popular and recorded a single that actually made the charts in Chicago. As they were on the verge of a national tour, with The Rolling Stones yet, Uncle Sam stepped in and grabbed them by the collars. Drafted. John and Allison thought if they signed up as regular army for three years, instead of the two as draftees, they would have their choice of jobs and have a kooshy tour of duty in the U.S. or maybe Germany. Naïve.

Allison, by the way, was also stationed with us in Korea. It was through him that John got into the entertainment outfit. But at the time of the meeting between John and me, Allison was on tour in Japan, the Philippines, and, ugh, Vietnam. The Travelers, the folk-rock group he performed in, had won an Army talent contest. The prize was a thirty-day working tour of those places.

By the time John finished unpacking, we were well on our way to being very good friends.

The following week was spent working on new choral pieces for the next General's Mess. John had a wide vocal range similar to mine and was also put in the tenor section.

Allison was due to arrive back soon, and John told me a little about his old home-town buddy and his double-jointed talent. John also mentioned that they planned to start a new band after they got out of the army, hopefully in the San Francisco Bay area. He asked if I'd be interested in being in the new band. Sure, I said, but I still wanted to be a cowboy and raise horses.

The Travelers were a four-piece folk-rock group with two guitars, a bass, and drums. They lived in the center of our u-shaped hootch not far from my area.

John, Allison, after he returned, and I hung out together, playing guitars and singing folk songs.

Two of the Travelers were about to turn out and fly back to the states to become civilians again, one guitarist and the bass player. John was scheduled to take the place of the guitarist. He and Allison asked if I wanted to be the new bass player. I'd never played bass before, but I agreed. How hard could it be? Only four strings instead of six.

Bill, the current bass player, had sent home for his 1957 Fender Precision bass but didn't want to deal with shipping it home again. He sold it to me for $50, extremely cheap for a classic guitar that could be worth around $15,000 today.

My pay as a Spec Four was about $100 a month, which was barely enough to buy zuzus at the PX. Spending $50 on an old Fender bass, would dip into my funds, but I really did like that guitar.

The bass player for the blues band, The Ground Floor People, Bobby, had played for a Texas group called Mother Earth, and was supposed to get back in that group when he got out of the army. (He did just that and recorded two albums and played the Fillmore and Avalon Ballrooms in San Francisco.) Bobby offered to teach me some bass playing techniques. For the next two weeks, before both bass players were to leave Korea, I was taught, and I practiced in the rehearsal hall for hours at a time.

Before I could become part of the Travelers, the variety show had a tour lined up. A train would take us from Seoul, to Taegu (Daegu), and then Pusan (Busan), on the southern tip of the Korean peninsula. Pusan was considered the Riviera of Korea. However, it was mainly a big navy base. The smaller army base where we were to stay was more of an R and R facility, kind of like RC#1. The tour was to last ten days, including the two to three days of train rides.

All the variety show members and all the instruments, sound and lighting equipment were piled in the big olive drab bus and headed for the Seoul train station. Everyone helped load the equipment in the baggage car, then boarded the passenger coach in front of it.

The train cars were old, but the seats were padded and fairly comfortable. Outside our passenger coach I could see all the other trains lined up for their destinations. Several were steam locomotives still fueled by coal, belching black smoke from their smokestacks. Our train was a newer American-made diesel.

Chuck sat next to me and told me that this train line was the South Korean part of the original Trans-Siberian railway. The Trans-Siberian rail line still ran from Moscow to North Korea, but after the tracks across the ImJim River had been blown up in the Korean War, the connection over the river to Seoul was no longer usable.

After eight hours of stop and go train travel, we reached our first destination, Daegu. After quickly unloading everything before the train pulled out again, an army bus picked us up and took us to the local army base.

The Daegu base was huge. It looked like there were a hundred tanks and an equal number of trucks lining the paved parking areas next to several large warehouse-sized machinist and mechanic facilities.

We unloaded our equipment and put it on the stage of a very large service club. A stern "donut dolly" in a blue special services uniform that fit her large and tall frame a little too tightly, making her boobs squeeze up and out and sitting too high on her body, directed us where to put our stuff. She then made a phone call to a sergeant who trotted over from the building next door to show us where we were to billet for the night: the guest hootch.

We were to start our show at 7:30 and had to be done and torn down by 9:30. By 6:30, the service club was nearly full already. I asked Nancy, the big donut dolly, how many the club held. Four hundred! I had never performed for a crowd that large. There were only a couple hundred chairs set up, but there were several sofas and easy chairs along the walls. Others stood against the walls in between the chairs.

Our show went over quite well. The white guys in the audience loved the white acts, including the two "hit" songs Billy, Mike and I sang, and the black guys loved the black soul groups. The band even did an encore, playing the Rascals' hit *Good Lovin'*.

As we started to tear down the equipment, we were inundated with questions and conversations by twenty or thirty soldiers. Several asked how they could get into the General's Chorus and play music all over Korea like we were doing. They didn't get an answer from us because Nancy walked between them, turned around and told them it was time to leave. She was taller than most of the guys and had an imposing stance and stare. Everyone quickly split.

The following day we traveled to Pusan where we were to do three shows on the Army and Navy bases. We had quite a bit of free time that first day, so several of us headed into town for some sightseeing. Chuck, being a little over six feet tall and with that curly flaming red hair, quickly became the subject of stares from all the young Koreans hanging out by the department stores and restaurants. Someone said something like "Beatles", I think, and a bunch of high school age boys and girls began to come up and touch us. One thrust an autograph book at Chuck, who acted like he really was a famous person, and he took a pen and signed his name.

Mistake.

More kids started showing up to see what was going on, and quite a few began screaming and trying to get through to touch us. We started to move away, and they started chasing us, just like we were the Beatles in *A Hard Day's Night*.

They pursued us down the street and followed us into a department store. We ran up three flights of stairs and came out on the rooftop. Several stores had connecting walkways on the roofs, and we ran across to the next building. I looked back to see that the crowd had thinned to only a dozen or so laughing and giddily screaming kids. By the time we ran down another set of stairs to street level, only two or three kids were behind us.

A couple of us had had enough by then and headed back to the base. Chuck and a few others went out to try it again.

After lunch at the PX cafeteria, Mike, Billy and I headed to the base movie theater for a matinee showing of *The Dirty Dozen*. The theater was nearly full, and we sat behind a couple of cute young white girls who took an interest in us.

One of the girls was too interested…

Chapter 9
The Dependent

Part 1
It started in Pusan

In 1967 I had a short, though memorable, relationship with a dependent, a dependent I can still remember by image, personality, and events, but not by name.

In the armed forces, a dependent is a child in a serviceman's family. Most of us 60's draftees, though, thought of dependents as Army or Navy brats. They were the sons and daughters of the lifers, the career servicemen. However, the dependent of my story was not just any ordinary dependent. She was a "Navy brat". She was the dependent of a high-ranking Naval officer. She was a Navy Admiral's Navy brat dependent who just happened to be very underage. Just looking at her could have put me in a military prison.

Yes, I remember nearly everything about her. I remember smiles, frowns, tears, and tantrums. I remember where everything happened and how it happened. I can remember longing for her and the pain I felt for that longing. I believe I even remember her scent: a childish, minty scent, like chewing gum. Yes, I remember her very well, but her name has sunk too far down into my gray matter. I'll never forget her, and I really do wish I could remember her name.

Actually, I did forget her, or rather *about* her, for a while. Shortly after I was discharged from the Army, I married. Having the responsibilities of marriage forced me to file away the still fresh memories of the dependent. And I really didn't want to think about her, or any other women, because my mind was so wrapped up in the uniqueness of matrimony. But now, as I get older, memories I had filed away in my subconscious begin to emerge in nostalgic surges. Recently, in one of these surges, the dependent, and all the associated pleasures and anxieties, re-entered my consciousness like a possessing spirit.

Her attachment to me tormented me for almost three months, but it easily aged me that in years. I can't blame her for the torment, though. I walked into that relationship willingly, with open arms and an open libido. I wanted affection, and I wanted to give her affection. I also wanted her out of my life. Why? Because not only did she cause me anxiety, due to her age and her actions, but I heaped guilt upon myself for thinking I betrayed the trust of the proverbial girl back home, the girl I later married.

This all started on that first trip down to Pusan, South Korea, with the variety show I was in. Our itinerary usually gave us time for recreation and sightseeing, and, the day after our first show, a few of us decided to go out to the base movie theater.

My friends and I naturally gravitated toward some round-eyes sitting together near the back of the theater. The term "round-eye" is GI slang for an enticing Caucasian female, a rarity in most of Korea. We sat down in some seats directly behind them.

Theater lighting isn't the best in the world for meeting girls; you never know what they really look like until it's too late. However, the girl in front of me seemed to radiate warmth that drew me to her. And as I leaned forward to try to initiate some conversation, I could see well enough that she was a very pretty, young woman. She said "Hi". first, and before the movie started, we were deep in a slightly nervous "getting-to-know-you" dialogue. Throughout the movie, we whispered back and forth cracking jokes about the plot and the characters.

Yes, she was cute. She looked all of eighteen and was more than eager to have verbal intercourse with me, as I was with her, verbal and otherwise. It seemed we were both very hungry for opposite-sex companionship. She gave me attention I voraciously consumed, and in return I gave her attention she seemed to ravenously crave.

In stature she was almost a head taller and much fuller figured than her friends, who seemed too young for her to be hanging around with. In the low lighting of the pre-feature, her hair appeared to be an eclectic blend of nearly every hair color I had ever seen. Depending on the way her head was turned, her hair could appear black, brunette, dark red, and sometimes almost blond. Her eyes were as interesting as her hair. They seemed almost light blue when I first looked into them, then later they seemed green. After the movie, and in the bright lights of the theater lobby, I noticed large flecks of green and brown on a background of blue; it was an unusual mixture that seemed unnatural to me, and one I've never seen since, but the uniqueness was just one more thing that attracted me to the girl.

Just before the lights dimmed for the movie, she stood up to take off her coat and exhibited a very mature-looking body artfully draped with a loose-fitting white cotton blouse styled similarly to a man's dress shirt. The sleeves were unbuttoned and rolled up almost to her elbows. The front was unbuttoned down far enough to tease me with a glimpse of cleavage. Her blouse was loosely tucked into a short-pleated skirt of navy blue and red plaid that ended just above her knees. The whole outfit reminded me of a Catholic school uniform.

When the movie ended and our two groups were in the lobby ready to say goodbye, she was quiet and a little fidgety. As her friends started to leave, she walked up to me, touched my arm, and nervously whispered in my ear that she would like to go for a walk. Of course, I said yes. And as soon as I said yes, a sudden anxiety almost overwhelmed me as my guilt-ridden mind drifted overseas to my girlfriend back home. I wanted this girl. I wanted to be with this girl. But I didn't want to betray my fiancée's trust.

The guilt wasn't strong enough to stop me, so we left the theater together. She left her friends, who looked a little disturbed at her leaving with me, and I left mine, who didn't care. We walked into the mild evening air talking about the movie and other slightly nervous, first date subjects. I did most of the talking at this point answering her questions about what I did in the variety show and how long I would be in Pusan.

Shortly, we found our way onto a bandstand in the middle of a small parade ground. Neither of us spoke now, and our self-conscious silence was disturbed only by the distant noises of the city. We leaned against the railing, side by side, and gazed toward a large hill behind Pusan.

We were close. Our arms kept touching, which caused me to nervously catch my breath a couple of times. Shortly, in the middle of a long, uncomfortable silence, I again caught my breath, touched her hand, then clasped it. Nearly the same time our fingers entwined, I pulled her around in front of me (or did she purposely circle around? I'm really not sure which), and she leaned into me. She looked straight and unblinking into my eyes as if she were trying to peer into my soul, then closed her eyes as she slowly, haltingly, tightened her embrace and lightly touched her lips to mine. After that first soft and tender kiss, her persona seemed to quickly change from a shy, unsure sexual novice to a forward, sexually experienced woman as she immediately pulled her whole body tighter into mine and kissed me again much harder. The third and all the uncounted succeeding embraces and kisses built with a feverish intensity toward a climax I felt might be embarrassingly premature as she pushed her body against my ever-growing member.

God, was she beautiful. God, did she feel good against me. God, was I horny. God, do you think she can feel the bulge in my pants? Oh, God.

"Ron?"

"Hmmmm."

"Ron?"

"Hm?"

"Ron, please stop."

She looked the novice again, releasing herself from my embrace, backing away but still holding my hands.

"Hmm? Uh...oh, I..I'm sorry," I said as my bulge receded to a slight crease. "I..I guess I was getting carried away."

"No. No, I'm afraid I was getting carried away. It's not your fault. I really wish we could get more carried away. But... But I've got to tell you something."

"You're married."

"No. I..."

"You're a Nun."

"Please. Don't joke," she said with a little edge in her voice. "Do you know how old I am?"

"Um, I thought women didn't like to have their ages known."

"Be serious with me," she almost snapped. "I... I'm only..."

"OK, you're at least eighteen or..."

"...fifteen."

"...nineteen?"

"Fifteen."

"Fifteen?"

"Fifteen."

"Nah."

Silence.

"Nah," I repeated. Then I continued with increasing nervousness, "No. No, you couldn't be..."

"I wish I wasn't, but I am. I... I'm grown up, though, more than everyone thinks. You thought I was eighteen, didn't you?"

Anxiety swept over me as I released her hands and stepped aside. My mind was reeling, and the dizziness brought on by my agitation caused me to turn away from her and grasp the handrail with both hands. My feelings for her, albeit mostly sexual at this point, were still strong and urged me, goaded me, to continue making love to her.   But this sudden turn of events made those feelings short circuit, leaving a very confused look on my face.

She moved back to my side and touched my arm, my back, my shoulder, the back of my head; she also seemed very confused about her feelings but did not want the momentum of our first encounter to die. I looked at her again and saw the taut lines of distress on her face, which must have mirrored my own expression.

"Please... please don't hate me," she said very quietly with a catch in her throat. She closed up the space between us and finally settled her nervous hands around one of mine, pulling it off the handrail and onto the center of her chest. The warmth of her body again drew me close to her. I relaxed my other hand, which was still on the rail, and felt my soul being invaded by her eyes again. I weakened. I turned and leaned against the railing once more.

"I... I really think I like you," she said almost inaudibly. In a whisper, she continued, hesitated, then finished, "I think... I love you."

I could barely hear her, but I could very easily read her lips. They formed the words slowly and distinctly, and her warm, sweet breath directed them into my face. I felt a lump form in my throat. She looked at me expectantly, obviously hoping for an equal or better expression of affection from me. I was drawn closer and wanted to say something in return, but no words formed that I could send back to her. I did almost kiss her again.

The headlights from a Jeep slowly circling around the parade ground flashed across the bandstand, illuminating the girl's face for a second. I saw, or thought I saw, the face of a very young child next to me. My mind reeled again and took me back into reality.

"But you look... I thought... I mean... you looked eighteen. Aren't you eighteen? Aren't you almost eighteen?"

Oh my God. My mind cleared enough to begin realizing the possible repercussions, and the more it soaked in the more I knew I was in trouble. One slip and it could be all over for me. I'd never see the good old U S of A again. I looked past her head and stared with half-focused eyes across the parade ground. All I could see was a vision of solitary confinement in a dark, dank, military prison. All I could think of was what would happen to me if her parents found out and what the Army would do to me if I got caught. I became very paranoid. Whereas I felt very alone with her on that bandstand just a few minutes before, I now thought the whole Army base was watching.

"Ron?"

Silence.

"Ron? Please look at me. Talk to me. I… I'm sorry. I should have told you sooner, but…"

"But what?" I finally said with a nervous tremor in my voice. I was shaking all over.

"I… I want to be with you. My friends act so young and immature. They really don't know what life, what love is about. I want to be with someone who will treat me like a grown-up woman. I am grown up. You can see that. You've been treating me like that. And besides, I…"

"What?"

"I'm really in love with you."

As she spoke, she looked directly into my eyes, and in the dimness, she again looked like a beautiful, innocent young woman. I could barely make out the tears flowing down her cheeks, but I saw well enough for them to cause me to soften and yearn for her once more. I felt like a moth attracted to an enticing flame and getting its wings singed in the process. My heart fluttered like the wings of that damaged moth, and I nearly fell as I stepped forward, took her in my arms and pulled her very close. Our lips automatically found each other, and we kissed one long and very gentle kiss. I tasted the damp saltiness of her tears as they continued to fall, trickling down her face and into our mouths.

She slowly pushed herself away from me and whispered in the voice of someone trying to be strong but on the verge of breaking down, "I.. I have to go...go home now. Please kiss me once more. Kiss me goodnight."

I did, several times, before she turned, stepped out of the bandstand, and broke into a run, quickly disappearing into the darkness at the edge of the parade ground. The taste of her tears was lingering on my lips as I passed my tongue over them, and it made me wish she was still kissing me. I felt good, momentarily. I felt wanted, and loved, momentarily. I felt like my fiancée didn't exist, momentarily. Momentarily, reality escaped me. But just for a moment.

For the next few days anxiety was my only companion. I shied away from my friends in the variety show and was barely able to concentrate on performing. My overactive mind tried to sort out, quite unsuccessfully, what had happened and how I could get out of it. I was extremely attached to my fiancée, but because she was half a world away and several months in my past, my memory of her was not fresh anymore. The newer memory of a bewitching young girl who lived so close and who I'd known only a few days invaded my older memories and kept me in a state of nervousness. I felt guilty for even considering being with another girl and betraying my fiancée's trust in me, and I felt anxiety-ridden and confused for falling for an underage high schooler barely out of puberty.

My nervousness lessened, though, because after a week I still had not heard from the girl. I relaxed and became more personable with my cohorts again. I felt the girl's sudden infatuation with me had cooled, and we'd probably never see each other again.

However, just before we were to leave Pusan, she came to the Army base on the pretext of doing schoolwork at the post library, but instead walked over to our quarters. She knocked on the door and Charlie, the variety show's drummer, answered. Shortly he came to my room. Billy and Mike, my two singing partners, were with me.

"Uh. There's a sweet young thing at the door a'lookin' for 'a Ronnie'. Is there anybody by that name in here?"

"Yipes. It's her," I said rather hoarsely. "God, she's back. Oh Lord, save me."

By this time, my friends knew all about what had happened after the movie that night. Since I felt I'd never see her again, I had gone ahead and told them nearly everything about that evening. They were amused at first then agreed with me that she would never come back. I now looked to them for sympathy but got only sly smiles. Bill began chanting.

"If she were my daughter, I'd..."

Charlie and Mike quickly answered.

"What would you do, daddy?"

"If she were my daughter, I'd..."

"What would you do, daddy?"

"Cut it out guys," I broke in.

"If she were my daughter, I'd..."

"That's enough...please," I cut in again as I stood up and tried to look threatening.

"What would you do, daddy?"

I left the room, and they kept singing that Mothers of Invention song.

"I'd smother that girl in chocolate syrup and strap her on again."

Those pretty and moist eyes were once more in front of me as I greeted her at the door. She was on the verge of crying and her lips quivered as if she were holding back sobs. Feelings for her like I felt that night on the bandstand overpowered me, and her warmth drew me toward her once more. I stepped out of the barracks, took her hand in mine, and led her away. I wanted to get as far away from any prying eyes or chanting voices as I could.

We walked for about fifteen minutes until we came to a fence at the edge of the base. We sat down on a low, flat rock by a cliff overlooking the Sea of Japan. We had been silent the whole distance, just walking and holding hands.

She spoke first. Her voice sounded weak but her grip on my hand was strong.

"Ronnie, I'm sorry I haven't seen you. It's been hard for me to get out. I heard that..."

"After not hearing from you I thought you'd forgotten about me," I interjected.

"No. No, I'd never do that. Don't you understand? I just couldn't get away from home."

She went on to tell me that she had been grounded for getting home so late that first evening. Not returning when she was supposed to caused her parents to make angry, inquiring phone calls to her friend's parents. They quickly found out her friends returned without her, and each friend, trying to protect her, had a different story. Her parents called the Shore Patrol, and a search was initiated. When she finally did return, it was in a Korean taxi that dropped her off far enough away from the gate for her to sneak in without being seen. It seems the local dependents had a secret hole cut through a secluded section of fence for purposes just like this. Unfortunately for her, it was after one o'clock in the morning. Not only was the Shore Patrol out hunting for her, but there was a military curfew at midnight. When she walked into her house, her mother, father, and two Shore Patrol officers were there to greet her. She didn't tell me what happened after that except that she was grounded.

"You see, I couldn't go out. I couldn't use the phone or anything," she said, seeming to plead for me to understand her. "Ronnie, I've thought about you a lot. I had to see you before you head North again. You've been the only one that has ever treated me like a grown-up. You really treat me like a woman. I like that. And I know I can trust you."

"How can you say that?" I asked a little too forcefully. My mind had suddenly filled with images of my fiancée, disappointed in me and saddened over my little escapade, and of this girl next to me, with the possible prison term I could get for what I'd like to do. I tried to continue talking without sounding upset.

"Look. You don't even know me. You know nothing about me."

"I know enough. You're nice to me." She was pleading again. "You treat me right. You seem to care about me." She paused, then quietly, in a very pained tone, said, "Don't you want to be with me?"

"Well..yes," I said, hesitantly. And my hesitation caused her face to contort into a more pained expression.

"You don't, do you," she cried.

"Yes, I do," I snapped back. The words slipped out before I could gather my thoughts. When I thought I was back on track again, I continued, "But you've got to look at reality. You know I'm leaving soon, all the way up north, several hundred miles away. You've got to realize I may never be able to come down here again."

"But you've got to come back," she said with accelerating distress. "I want to keep seeing you. I want to be with you."

Feelings akin to panic flowed through my whole body. I took a couple of deep breaths and grew slightly dizzy. Maybe, I thought, I could just hyperventilate, pass out, and when I awoke, she'd be gone. No, I can't escape it. I took another deep breath and continued.

"Please. Come on now. I've got to leave. I'm in the Army. They expect me to go where they send me. I am leaving tomorrow morning, and there's nothing we can do about it."

"You can't. I haven't seen you enough. It's not fair," she screamed, shocking me by the outburst and causing me to glance around to make sure no one heard. "Why can't anything good happen to me? I hate it. I hate my life."

I didn't know what to say. She quickly rose to her feet and paced around me, her hands clenched and her feet kicking up clouds of dust.

"Why can't good things last for me?" she continued asking. I didn't know if she was asking me, herself, or some deity, since she was looking, and yelling, into space. "God, I hate my life. I hate it here. I hate my parents. I hate everything."

It was analyst time.

"Please. Please relax," I said as calmly as I could under the circumstances. I thought I'd try the standard "real-life-is" lecture. "Look. Real life has all kinds of ups and downs. It doesn't always have a happy ending that lasts forever like that movie we saw when we first met. It would be impossible for us to be together all the time right now."

She began to yell something back at me. I quickly raised my hand to stop her. I saw my lecture wasn't working. "Maybe," I choked out, taking the coward's way out, "we can write to each other. I want to keep in touch. Then if I don't make it back here to Pusan again, we can meet in the states when I'm out of the Army. I've got around seven more months, which isn't that long, you know. And you did say you'll be returning to California when you leave Korea. We could meet there or something."

I was grasping at straws to calm her down. What started as a lecture on how hard life can be was ending up as more assurances of a continuing romance. It was working, though. She sat back down next to me and looked at her feet. In the short silence, more images of my fiancée flashed through my mind and the possible conflict back home. My train of thought almost derailed.

"Yeah. We can write each other. Who knows? Maybe I'll be back here in Pusan in a few months for another tour. We could see each other again then."

I had no idea where it would go from that point. There I was sitting next to a very beautiful, very grown-up looking fifteen-year-old girl who had just scared the bejeezus out of me with her tantrum and made me want to get away from her as fast as possible. Now I felt her warmth once more and it attracted me. I was holding her hand again and thinking about making love to her.

God was I torn. I wanted to tell her our relationship wouldn't work and that she should forget me. And now looking at her in the dim evening light, I also wanted to tell her I loved her, which I had never done to any girl except my fiancée. In a selfish way, I did love her. I loved her because she was there, and I was lonely. I loved her because I really did want our relationship to advance beyond kissing and handholding.

The paranoia I felt because of her age kept me from saying it. But my paranoia didn't keep me from putting my finger under her chin and directing her lips toward mine. That much was inevitable. The attraction was too strong to resist. Her kisses were so soft and yet full-mouthed and intense. There was an incredible tenderness in the touch of her lips that implied innocence yet screamed experience. I closed my eyes and tried to lose myself in the feelings. I lost track of everything when our lips met. Except time. My noisy old Timex was close to my ear when I wrapped my arms around her. The ticking seemed out of place in the middle of a romantic interlude and it quickly brought me back to awareness. I gave her another slow kiss then whispered that I had to go.

The variety show had one more concert that night, and I had to get back to the barracks. I figured that when we said goodbye this time it would be the last we would ever get to see each other. I was sure she was thinking the same, so I told her otherwise.

My reassurances that we would see each other again someday didn't seem to placate her at all. She cried all the way back to the barracks and refused to say goodbye. She wanted real promises. She wanted commitments.

Finally, Billy called out for me to come in and get ready for that night's show. His voice broke the spell and saved me from saying any more things I might be sorry for later. She gave me a quick kiss and walked away. I couldn't watch. I had a lump in my throat about the size of a basketball, and I felt moisture building up in my eyes. I closed the door and walked back to my room. Billy and Mike were there.

"If she were my daughter, I'd..."

"What would you do, daddy?"

She wrote daily, for a few days, then the letters dropped to about one a week. I hoped she had cooled off a bit with my not being around her, but her letters were still peppered with sad, loving sentiments and innocently suggestive promises. She succeeded in seducing me into wanting to see her again.

Yes, I got seduced, in more ways than one. Her suggestive, albeit naive, advances toward me on paper were, unfortunately, similar to the ones I received from my fiancée. I was having pretend sex with two girls I couldn't touch. But with the one in Pusan closer and fresher in my mind, I fantasized more about her. If you can't be with the one you love, love the one you're with.

I wrote, as I promised, at least once a week and purposely kept from saying anything that might be taken as a promise of love. I thought I was slowly weaning her away from me. But, in her mind, just the fact of my writing was taken as that promise.

Part 2
The Mother

About three months later, I was on the road again, this time with the Army touring group I had recently joined, the folk-rock band called The Travelers.

I wrote to the girl telling her when I'd be in Pusan again, and I expected her to be waiting for me when I got off the bus. She wasn't there, and there were no messages. I thought she might have gotten herself grounded again, or locked in her room, or something worse.

We arrived about four in the afternoon to set up our equipment at the Pusan Naval Base Officer's Club. As soon as I walked into the club, I was told by a Korean servant that a lady wanted to see me. He took me to the lady's table.

With no introduction, I knew right away that she was the girl's mother. And what a mother she was! I observed from the number of lipstick-stained cigarette butts in the ashtray that it looked as if she had been in the club since opening or at least most of the day. And by the way she held on to her glass, also lipstick stained, I thought she might have had as many drinks as cigarettes. She looked plastered.

Although I could see a resemblance to her daughter, her alcoholic state pretty much wiped away any beauty that she might have shared with her child. Her face was slightly wrinkled and had a tanned, leathery look about it. Too much sun and too much leisure time, I thought. Her eyes were watery and bloodshot, and her eyeliner was smeared. She could have been taller than her daughter, but her bent-over inebriated posture kept me from making a comparison. On her thin frame she was wearing a rather short tight-fitting dress that looked a little too cheap for the locale. It forced cleavage where none was supposed to be, and exposed portions of her breasts that were also tanned, slightly wrinkled, and leathery. In fact, as I took in more of her, all her exposed parts, her arms, legs, and thighs, were like that. I have always been fairly open minded, but the amount of flesh she was exposing was too much for the time and place. I wondered if her daughter would look like this someday.

Without looking at me, she motioned with a wave of her hand for me to sit down. She held up her glass, moved it around in a slightly erratic circular motion so the ice clinked against the sides, and stared into it, or maybe she went into a coma.

After several uncomfortable minutes, and without introducing herself, she put her glass down and spoke, her alcohol-tinged breath nearly pushing me away from the table.

"You know my daughter's San Quentin quail?"

"I beg your pardon?"

"My daughter. She's San Quentin quail. She's underage. Jailbait, mister."

I was speechless. I didn't know how to react. She took a quick drink of something green with a wrinkled, red maraschino cherry in it. It was hard to compose myself.

"Yes ma'am," I nearly whispered. "I know that. I didn't when I met her, though, she looks much older than she is..."

"And that goddamn little bitch probably told you she was older," she slurred and shot back at me, spraying a little of her drink along with her words. A few heads at other tables turned to watch us.

"You know that little brat gives me all kinds of hell," she continued, a little quieter. She now seemed to be talking to herself. "So young but trying to act so grown up. She'll probably end up getting in trouble like all girls her age. When I was her age..." She looked down at her drink in front of her and seemed to reflect on something. She never finished her sentence.

"Do you like her?" She almost yelled, taking me by surprise and causing a few more heads to turn.

86

"Uh, yes. Very much."

"Do you want her? No, no. I mean… I mean are you honorable? You look honorable, even if you are Army and need a haircut." She paused, took another drink, then said, "Take good care of her, son. Take my little girl and be good to her." She paused, then shook her finger at me and said, "But, you know, if you hurt her, you'll have to answer to me. You'll have to answer to me."

In her state she didn't sound too convincing as a caring mother. But the more she spoke, the more I was beginning to catch on to what she inferred. She wanted her daughter out of her way. There was obviously domestic friction between mother and daughter, and she wanted someone to take her little girl off her hands. I just happened to be convenient.

"You are good looking," she mumbled as she took another drink. "Too bad I didn't see you first."

She shifted in her chair and leaned across the table. She brought her breasts down upon her folded arms, obviously trying to show more cleavage and trying to be more seductive. She only succeeded in nearly folding her boobs right out of her dress. Her cigarette smoke and liquor-tinged breath hit me again as I swallowed hard and felt my stomach attempt to not accept my swallow. My eyes didn't want to accept what I was seeing either. I was repulsed. Unfortunately, she reached out and took my hand before I could retract it.

"Just take care of her," she said, squeezing my hand a little too hard. "Take good care of her. My husband, the… the Admiral, asked me to tell you... something. Now... I don't remember what it was. Dammit to hell anyway."

"The Admiral? Her father's an Admiral?"

"Of course. Runs this god-damned base...all shit… ship shaped. He's a right-fine old bugger too. Cut quite a figure in his day. He's attached to his daughter, so you'd better be careful."

She then said almost inaudibly and into her glass as she started to take another drink, "Maybe too attached."

She lowered her glass and her voice trailed off. She stared straight at me. Through most of our conversation she had been talking to the bottom of her glass and at the table top. I felt really uncomfortable with her looking at me until I noticed that her eyes were pretty glazed over. She wasn't staring at me, she was staring through me, deep in drunken thought.

"I really must go," I said, trying to get her attention back to earth and my hand out of hers and back to myself. "I have to go to work now."

"Huh? Oh. Well...you look like a real nice boy." She blinked her eyes as if waking up, patted my hand, then let go. "I think you'll be a fine match for my little girl. Have her write her mother once in a while. OK?"

I didn't answer her. She didn't look like she was waiting for one since she was again staring at the table top. She seemed to think her daughter and I were already engaged and walking down the aisle.

I pushed back my chair and excused myself, leaving her there clasping her glass with both hands. I went outside to help finish unloading the equipment. When I returned, she was gone. All that remained was a lipstick stained empty glass with a very wrinkled, red maraschino cherry in it. I didn't see her leave, and I never saw her again.

Her last words echoed in my ears: "Have her write her mother once in a while." That gave me the impression that the girl must have told her mother that I had asked her to marry me. All of a sudden, my future had been planned out for me and I didn't get invited to the organizing committee meeting.

The Travelers had to perform at other military compounds along the coastline for the next two days, which kept me from seeing the girl right away after that confrontation with her mother. For two days I could hardly concentrate on my work. I was restless and slept very little. Things had gone too far with the girl, but I couldn't see how. I only kissed her. I had made no promises.

The day we returned to Pusan from our short trip, we found her waiting in front of our building, sitting on the doorstep of our guest quarters. We all said "uh-oh" in unison as our bus pulled up.

"Ronnie. You're back. You're back," she said loud enough to hear over the bus's engine. She ran up to the side of the bus and reached up to me through the open window before the bus had stopped. I gave her a weak smile, and she ran to the door and waited for me to get off. I glanced back at my friends and my look of despair brought out only shrugging shoulders and half-assed smiles from them. I got off the bus.

"Yeah, I'm back," I said rather curtly, trying to show my annoyance to them and to her. The others got off the bus, circled around us, and went into the barracks, chuckling. I looked back at her and her face looked like I had just slapped her. She drew back, turned away, covered her face with her hands, and cried.

Oh, no, my weakness again. It always hurts me to see someone unhappy when I think it's because of me or something I said. I tend to say anything to cheer them up even if it means worse trouble later. My mouth can get pretty stretched out from putting my foot in it so often.

I put my hands on her shoulders and whispered in her ear.

"I'm sorry. I'm really sorry. It's just been a rough tour so far," I lied. "We're all a little grouchy right now," I lied again. We had actually been having a great time. "I'm sorry if it sounded like I was snapping at you, but I've been working really hard, and I'm really tired," I lied two more times.

"Ronnie," she breathed quietly and sweetly into my face. "I'm leaving in a couple of weeks. I'm going back to the states. My parents are sending me away."

Her mother must have sobered up enough to realize what she had said to me.

"Where are they sending you?"

"To my grandmother's in Chicago. I'm being sent away. I won't be able to see you anymore." Her voice got louder and was on the brink of hysteria again. Instead of hysterics, though, she stopped talking, put her arms around me, and buried her face in the side of my neck and sobbed.

I was actually beginning to feel relief. She was going away, and not to California. This meant she couldn't be a threat to my relationship with my fiancée. At least that's what I thought at that moment.

"Ronnie?"" she finally said after several minutes of crying. "Isn't there somewhere we can go to be alone? Somewhere no one can see us?"

"Not here. There's no really private place on an Army base."

"How about our bandstand--after dark."

"Yeah, I suppose, if no one walks by. Yeah, it is dark there and sort of private. Why?"

She held me extremely tightly, put her lips to my ear and whispered things she had only innocently hinted at in her letters.

"I… I want you to take me. I want you more than anything. Make love to me. Please. I want you inside of me."

No no no no no no no! I thought in wide-eyed, rapid-fire silent exclamation as I tried to push away from her. *This won't do. I can't. There's no way I'll ever do that. But... I want her.*

And I pulled myself closer to her. *No no no no no no no. I can't think about it.*

I'm still a virgin, but my ever-increasing horniness could be my undoing here. I was fighting with myself, trying to persuade myself out of even considering what she suggested. But her closeness was a severe detriment.

Unfortunately, my immediate reaction was to get an erection, which I was sure she could feel since she was so tightly pressed against me. I winced. And I throbbed.

"B..but," was all I could get out of my mouth. She stifled my words with her lips. God, did I want her.

"Ronnie, I hate to leave. Oh, how I really hate to leave. But if I don't report home shortly, I can't go out tonight. My mother thinks I'm going to the movies with some friends. God, she treats me like a little girl. I'll try to sneak back here after dark."

Oh great.

She again pressed herself against me as tightly as possible and kissed me, very passionately. I was sure I felt her thrust her hips forward into mine a couple of times. My erection got painfully hard and was trapped downward in my underpants. It fit quite naturally between her legs right where she had pushed.

"God. I've really got to go," she said as she seemed to nervously pull back and looked at her watch, then in sort of a distracted way looked down at the bulge in my pants. "God. I've really got to go." She gave me one more quick kiss and trotted away. I sat down on the doorstep so my erection wouldn't hurt so much and began daydreaming, and worrying, about our upcoming encounter. I didn't hear John, our guitar player, come up behind me.

"I can't believe she's only fifteen," he said, shocking me by his presence and shocking me back to reality.

Yes, she was only fifteen. She was fifteen and wanted to make love to me. I, at 21, was still a virgin. I took it for granted she still was too. Also, I promised my fiancée that I would save myself for her when we were married. And now, thoughts about my fiancée were bringing on guilt which invaded and lessened my lust. Then duty intervened and invaded guilt.

"Oh my God, John. I can't see her tonight."

"Of course, you can't. We've got a gig tonight."

"We've got a gig tonight! Oh my God. She made me completely forget that. I don't have any way of telling her."

"Why don't you call her at her home?"

"I can't. I might get her mother or father. I definitely don't want to talk to them. Oh Christ!"

"Think of it this way, Ron, maybe she'll get the hint and stop bothering you. And believe me, you've been pretty bothered ever since you met her," he said, tapping my head with his index finger.

"I don't want to hurt her, though."

"Then write to her when we get back to RC One," John said a little curtly. I could see he was getting impatient with me. "That's only a few days from now."

"Yeah, I can do that. But I wish there was some way to tell her now."

"This will keep you from getting yourself into serious trouble," John said as he gave me a pop on the head with the butt of his hand.

John was right. A rendezvous with the girl would be disastrous. What if she freaked out and cried rape or something? What if she got pregnant? What if I try to leave her and she got mad and had me busted? And what if she decided to never let me go and did come out to California? Yeah, John was right. I could get into very serious trouble.

It was nearly midnight when we returned from our performance, and there was no sign of the girl. She was not waiting for our bus and there was no note pushed under the door to our barracks. In fact, I didn't see or hear from her again during our last few days in Pusan.

I did write her before we left and again when I got back to RC#1 trying to explain what happened. Since I didn't get an answer, I felt pretty secure that it was all over between us.

Back north at RC#1, the dull days dragged by until they combined to make a long, boring week. I still had five months left to my tour of duty, and I lazed around stoned on my bunk a lot more than I used to. I was thinking about home and about making love to my fiancée. I often had daydreams that revolved around the possible greetings I might get at the airport, the possible lovemaking that was ahead, and the hope for a Utopian existence with no worries, no hassles, and no money problems: dreaming the impossible dream; the American dream. I spent a lot of time lying on my bunk with my hands behind my head and my eyes half closed, smoking joints.

One afternoon after band rehearsal, I returned to my pipedreams, and was about to nod off when I was tapped on the shoulder.

"Uh, hey, Ron," Billy, one of the newer entertainers and our new drummer, said, in a rather halting voice. He looked a little nervous. "Are you awake? Uh...well, there's someone here asking for you."

"Huh? Really? I wonder who..."

I never completed my question. Into the building, a building with at least 35 healthy, young, lustful soldiers, came two very good-looking young girls: my young problem child and a very nervous-looking friend of hers. When the girl saw me, she left her friend standing in the doorway and ran to me, knelt down by my bunk, took my hand, and, again, started crying.

Word spread fast. The entire building funneled its male population into my area. Everyone wanted to see the pretty round-eyes. The girl at my side didn't notice the crowd and kept crying. I looked at everyone with wide, panic-stricken eyes. The other girl had come in and was standing uncomfortably against the wall behind her friend. She was consciously moving her feet from side to side and rubbing the sole of one shoe over the top of the other, scuffing the already well-scuffed finish. With her feet in constant movement, she looked like she was ready to walk out of there on a moment's notice. She was another of those young girls that had recently crossed over, quite successfully, into womanhood, and also could have passed for eighteen. Her blond hair partially covered her eyes. They looked as wide as mine and as full of panic. She kept glancing around to all the faces that stared at her, then glanced at the floor, then glanced again to all the faces. She constantly rubbed imaginary wrinkles out of the front of her white blouse and the sides of her tight light blue stretch Levi's. The poor girl was definitely scared. So was I.

After what seemed like hours, but couldn't have been more than a few minutes, I started to get over my initial shock and passed into stark panic as I thought about getting caught with two runaway dependents in my charge. Something needed to be done before any officers or NCO's found out that the girls were here.

Our little compound was only about three miles from the DMZ and was in an area restricted to almost all American civilians. It was definitely restricted to dependents. There were no wives or children of servicemen north of Seoul. If these girls got caught, they would be in serious trouble. If I got caught harboring these girls, I would be spending the next twenty years in a military prison.

"Ron. Uh, Ron," John said, trying to get my attention. When my mind cleared a little and I looked up at him, he continued, "We've got to hide these girls somewhere until we figure out how to get them out of here."

My sobbing young teen looked up at John in a rather startled way.

"Why? Why can't I stay here somewhere? I've brought money. I can stay in that village outside in a hotel."

"Listen," I said, trying to compose myself. "There are no hotels in this village--at least none that rent rooms on more than an hourly basis. And if there were hotels, you couldn't stay in them because you're a dependent. You're an underage American dependent. You're not allowed up here."

She buried her face in my chest and kept crying. Between sobs she tried to speak.

"You don't want me? You don't want me here?"

"Can't you understand what I'm saying? It's against the law for you even to be north of Seoul. And... how did you get up here?" I directed the question at the other girl who was pressed even harder against the wall, trying to keep distance between herself and the crowd that was moving in closer to her. I didn't know if she heard me, so I asked again. She didn't raise her head but spoke to me through her hair that was now almost totally covering her face "Uh...oh. We took the train to Seoul. Then...then we found a cab driver that could speak English and had him drive us here. He said nothing about it being against the law for us to be here."

"He wouldn't. All he wanted was your money. But how did you get in the gates?"

"We just walked in. The MP at the gate was arguing with some Korean and wasn't looking our way at all.

"Jesus! There must have been at least a hundred soldiers between the gate and here that saw you walk over here!" I said quickly and nervously. "We could get caught any minute. Hey, someone watch the doors!"

A few guys went to the doors and windows and watched in the direction of the company office and the officers' and NCOs' barracks. No one was headed our way.

"Why don't we smuggle them over to the entertainment center until we can sneak them out," John asked the rest of the guys. "Maybe after dark."

I released myself from the girl's grasp and got up. She stayed on her knees and looked at me with watery eyes.

"Let's get them into some fatigues so they won't stand out so much," I said, grabbing an extra shirt and pants out of my locker. "Anyone got another pair?"

John tossed a shirt and pants on the bunk.

"Put these on over your clothes," I told the girls. "Several of us will walk over in a group with you two in between us. We'll go along the fence, so we don't run into any officers or sergeants." Then I turned to the girl and quietly spoke to her. "Once we get over there, we'll have time to talk privately about...us."

She acted satisfied with that, wiped her eyes, stood up, and put on the fatigues over her tight Levi's.

"They need some boots," I said to no one in particular. Several pairs were immediately brought over. The girls chose the smallest pairs and put them on. I showed them how to blouse their pant legs into the boots.

A couple of hats were brought over, and the girls tucked as much hair as they could under them.

They still looked too much like girls, but we had to take a chance.

Two guys ran on ahead to check on the building to make sure no officials were there. One came back and told us the coast was clear. The other kept a lookout at the building.

A dozen of us left the barracks by a side door and walked in a tight group around the girls. We made our way along the outside fence for a short distance staying out of sight and away from the busier areas of the compound. Unfortunately, between us and the entertainment building was a large concrete drainage ditch. To get to the closest crossing, a narrow wooden pedestrian bridge, we had to cut back toward the main area.

As we neared the bridge, I saw our lookout about a hundred yards away wave frantically and point in our direction. No sooner had I seen his gestures than around the corner of a building right next to us came Lieutenant Bowman with one of the service club hostesses.

We stopped dead in our tracks.

"Good day, Sir!" Allison, the Travelers' rhythm guitar player, yelled, snapping to attention with an exaggerated salute, as was his sarcastic custom around officers he didn't care for. We all stood at attention and saluted with shaking hands. The girls wisely copied our actions.

"Good...good day, men," Lieutenant Bowman replied, a little nervous himself. "Are you going to the hall to rehearse?"

"Yes sir," several of us responded at once. I noticed a look of disappointment cross the lieutenant's face.

"Well, I was going to show Miss Pryor, who's new with the Service Club, our facilities," he said to us, "but I don't want to disturb your work. We'll see it later. Carry on, men."

We saluted, the girls saluted, the lieutenant saluted, and Miss Pryor smiled at us and nodded. The lieutenant then grabbed Miss Pryor by the arm and headed back the way they came.

That was easy.

Lieutenant Bowman seemed more nervous than usual and never looked directly at us. We turned and nearly ran across the bridge.

Once inside the entertainment building, I took the girl into a storage room where we could be alone. John and Allison took the other girl backstage and out of sight. The rest of the guys stood guard.

I sat her down on a speaker cabinet and squatted down in front of her with her hands in mine. Tears formed in her eyes again and trickled down her cheeks.

"I know I shouldn't have come," she spoke first. "I had to see you again before I left for America. I needed to find out if you are really serious about me."

Again, words seemed to stick in my throat. I didn't want to lie to her and make promises about our possible future, but her tears made me want to make those promises. But those promises scared me. I had to keep telling myself that she was only fifteen. She was, like her mother said, San Quentin quail.

I shook off the vision of prison and decided to be honest with her, brutally honest if necessary.

"Look," I finally got out of my mouth. "I like you a lot. In fact, I think about you constantly. But you're going home soon, and I've still got a little while to go here in Korea. You're young and pretty and there's a real good chance that you'll meet and...and fall for another guy in whatever school you end up going to. In a few months you'll forget about me and..."

"No," she cut in sharply. "I'll never love anyone else. I've always wanted you. I'm not a fickle little girl with a puppy-love crush like you and everyone else seems to think. I'll never, ever love anyone else. How can you say I'll meet someone else? I won't look at another guy. I want you."

She stomped her feet like a child throwing a tantrum. I felt frustrated that I couldn't get myself, or my feelings, across without causing scenes and felt a little hysteria of my own coming on. I suppressed it and decided on another tack.

"Let me finish," I cut in, using a tight-jawed authoritarian tone that emphasized each word. "I do like you. I like you a lot and I'd hate to see you go with someone else. And I don't think you're a fickle little girl. OK? So, let's keep writing, huh? If you still feel the same about me when I get home, we can take it from there. When the time comes that we might be able to see each other in the states, you'll have had some time to think about your future, and if you'll want to spend it with me. You'll be older and wiser."

That cliché hurt when I said it, but what really hurt was the look she gave me.

"You do think I'm a child," she said, in the same type of tight-jawed, authoritarian tone I had been using. "Stop treating me like one. Goddamn it. You're treating me like my parents do. I'm grown up. I am grown up."

She then became very quiet and stared off at the wall behind me. After nearly fifteen minutes of uncomfortable silence, with her barely moving and my watching her tight jaws grinding away on her teeth, I stood up and spoke.

"It's starting to get dark outside. We've got to get you and your friend out of here before you're discovered."

She didn't seem to be listening. She just looked at me like a tight-mouthed, pouting, rebellious child that had been severely scolded by an adult and resented the adult for it. We were silent again for several minutes. We just stared at each other.

The tears had stopped. She looked away from me and stared into the corner of the small room and seemed to be thinking. She looked a little more relaxed. At last she blinked, straightened up, and wiped the remaining tears off her cheeks.

"OK," she said, her voice rather strong for a young girl just going through an emotional crisis. "I'd better get back to Pusan right away. How can we get out of here?"

"Uh, there's a side gate you can sneak out," I replied, a little shocked by her change. "The lifeguard for the pool across the road lives in our building. That gate leads to the pool. He's got a key. We can wait there for a cab to come along then get you and your friend on your way."

"Good," she said as she stood up and headed for the door. "Let's go."

I was prepared for more emotion. I wasn't prepared for the sudden coldness. My change in tact, which I thought would placate her and cause things to continue as before, instead seemed to change her from a crying, spoiled child to a strong, independent woman, a side of her that attracted me to her all the more. I momentarily forgot about her age, her running away from home, and my fiancée. I saw before me someone I wouldn't mind spending the rest of my life with, or at least the rest of my time in Korea.

Now I was looking forward to farewell hugs and kisses, in fact I was hoping for hugs and kisses, but reality quickly returned when I had to hurry to the door ahead of her to see if it was safe to go out. It was.

The sun had set behind the mountains, and the long twilight time of these deep valleys was just beginning. It would be nearly two hours before it was completely dark. We still had to be careful.

I called the others together and explained the plan. One of the guys headed off in search of the lifeguard. They both returned within ten minutes.

In another five minutes all of us were grouped around the girls once more and headed back across the compound toward the side gate.

Before we reached the bridge, though, I again saw one of our lookouts wave frantically at us. I knew what to expect this time. Lieutenant Bowman and Miss Pryor came around the corner, like before, on their way to the rehearsal hall. We got out of there just in time. We all saluted as we noisily tromped across the old wooden structure and kept walking. I glanced at the lieutenant and saw a smile cross his lips as the two of them turned toward the hall and started over the bridge.

We made it to the gate, and all gathered around to shield the lifeguard while he unlocked the padlock. Opening that gate any time other than for official purposes was a breach of regulations that could have had all of us court-martialed and sent to infantry outfits on the DMZ. There was still enough light for us to be seen from a good distance, so we had to be extremely careful.

The lifeguard quietly removed the chain that held the gate to the fence post. We stood there for what seemed like hours for an empty cab to come by. Nearly all of them had soldiers in them. Finally, we saw an empty cab coming, and I swung the gate open and flagged it down. The girls were right behind me. Several hands reached out and quickly shut the gate after us.

"Do you have money for the cab?" I asked the girl.

"Of course, I do," she said rather tersely. These were the first words she had spoken since we left the hall. "Do you still think I'm a little kid? I'm grown up. I came prepared. For everything!"

Her paradoxical personality shifts between woman and child came rather abruptly. Now her tone was more like a pouting child again. This must be the way she spoke to her own parents; *the real her*, I thought. *Maybe it's better she's out of my life after all.*

The two girls leapt into the cab. The other girl looked across to me and said goodbye. My girl looked straight ahead and said nothing. Her jaws were again tight and grinding away at her teeth. I waved and got no response. The cab headed down the dirt road in a cloud of dust.

I stood there and watched the cab disappear around a turn and would have stood there longer if John hadn't opened the gate and pulled me back into the compound. He had seen an MP's jeep headed down the road toward us. It passed by without slowing down.

Once I was back inside, the others quietly dispersed leaving me alone with my thoughts. I clung to the fence and stared down the road watching the dust settle. I had a pretty good-sized lump in my throat, but I felt that a very large weight had been taken off my shoulders.

I must have stood by the gate for ten minutes or more until I noticed that some clouds had filled the sky and it had become windy and cool. I took a relieving, deep breath of the charcoal-smoke scented air and made a heavy audible sigh. Yes, I felt relieved. And sad.

Turning to walk back into the barracks, a movement in the direction of the rehearsal hall caught my attention. In the distance I could just make out Miss Pryor popping out of the rehearsal hall door with Lieutenant Bowman directly behind her. He was fastening his belt and making frantic apologetic gestures, spreading his arms in "forgive me" fashion. He tried to step in front of her and got roughly pushed out of the way. He then turned and slowly walked back into the hall, his head down and his hands in his pockets.

No, I never heard from her again. After all she put me through, the pleasure, the pain, the concern, and the general uneasiness, and after all the confusion she must have suffered in that dangerous, adolescent, almost-a-woman mind of hers, she just disappeared off the face of the earth, or at least out of my life.

Three weeks after putting her into that cab, I was on another performing tour of Korea and back in Pusan. I couldn't stop thinking about the girl. Again, on our first night there, I went to the movies at the base theater. There was no one to ask about her. I sat in the same seat but found only noisy children sitting in front of me where my talkative woman-child had sat that first night. After the movie, and during several of the following evenings, I walked to the places where we had our little rendezvous and succeeded only in finding depression. She was gone. It finally hit me. I would never see her again.

But I'll never forget her.

I just wish I could remember her name.

Chapter 10
The Travelers

While my dependent psychodrama was in the middle of its lifecycle, I transferred from the variety show to the folk-rock group, The Travelers. Bill, the previous bass player was leaving within the week and John and Allison asked if I'd like to take over on bass and vocals.

I moved all my clothes, my bedding, and my kimchi stand to the central part of our u-shaped hootch where John, Allison and Billy, the drummer, were located. I shared a corner area with John separated by wall lockers and a large kimchi stand. The lockable big kimchi stand that Allison had built in the wood shop on base, was as tall as the wall lockers and housed a stereo, two reel-to-reel tape recorders, a record player and two speakers. Allison had set up headphone jacks at each of our beds so we could lie in bed and listen to music late at night without bothering anyone else.

Allison was unique. He was double jointed and was often called The Gargoyle, because he would get on top of a wall locker, put his legs around his neck, and stretch his face in a wild wide-mouth, big-eyed gargoyle leer, rocking his body back and forth on his hands. He did this once while Top, our paranoid, gun-toting, first sergeant came into the building to harass us, looked up and saw Allison, freaked and ran out of the building. Top seldom came into our hootch after that.

Allison was a funny guy, but often with a biting humor. He had a slightly caustic personality with everyone except his old friend John. They both came from the same New Jersey town and had been in bands together. Allison told John about the entertainment outfit, so John had requested to be stationed at RC#1 after he came to Korea.

Allison had already been in Korea over a year, applied for an extension to stay at RC#1 and got it so he and John could play music together again. Not long after he first came to Korea, he had received a letter from home telling him his fiancée was killed in an auto accident. Some woman's dog jumped into her lap while driving and she lost control of her car, broadsiding Allison's girlfriend's car. She died instantly. John told me that Allison's personality changed after that, and you could tell there was sadness behind his gargoyle posturing and joking.

The rehearsals began right away after I moved in. I had to learn my bass and vocal parts to at least fifteen songs for two sets in the Traveler's next gig in a week. Fortunately, all the songs were ones I knew from records and the radio. We worked on some Beatles, Byrds, and Jefferson Airplane pieces. My bass technique improved daily.

Our first show was in our own service club on a packed Saturday night. Since I used to play and sing folk songs in front of people back home before I was drafted, I was not nervous at all when we went on stage. I just stood to the side, next to the drummer, and let John and Allison, in the front, on the left and right of me, do the introductions. I played along with the drummer's beat, sang some harmonies, and had a great time not thinking about being half a world away from home.

We were dressed in similar British-style Nehru-collar suits that a local tailor in the RC#1 PX made for us. In areas close to the DMZ no civies were allowed, but we could wear them while performing.

We rocked and rolled familiar songs we thought everyone could really enjoy. We finished our second set with a rousing version of the Jefferson Airplane's *Somebody to Love* and brought the audience to their feet applauding us.

The following week we had two shows. During the week we were scheduled to give a special goodwill show in Seoul at a Korean high school playing a short half-hour set in their auditorium, then on Friday, we were to play, for the first time, at the Peace Center in Panmunjom. We were a little nervous about traveling there because our driver/roadie would have to check out a gun for the trip and drive us up there in a barely running Special Services black Ford van.

The high school show was an eye opener. The special services lady who arranged the concert came with us to make sure everything went according to plan.

We were met at a loading ramp next to the auditorium by a Korean army colonel who spoke English quite well with hardly any accent. After discussing a few rules and regulations with our blue-uniformed liaison, he directed us through a door into the dressing room area behind the stage. We had an hour to set up and prepare for the short, half-hour lunchtime concert.

We were almost set up behind the closed curtain and could hear what sounded like hundreds of young voices on the other side.

As we turned on our amps and began to tune up, the hundreds of voices began cheering and screaming. We looked at each other and shrugged in a what-the-hell-is-going-on manner.

There were nearly five minutes before we went on, so after tuning, we went in our dressing room to change, use the bathroom (a hole in a concrete floor), and drink a little Coke before heading out for our gig.

Finally, our special services hostess and the colonel came in and said the auditorium was full and it was time to play.

I strapped on my bass, John and Allison strapped on their guitars, and Billy sat down behind his drums. The curtain opened.

Christ! The auditorium was a gigantic cement structure with what seemed like a thousand seats in front of the stage and another thousand in two balconies. The seats were full of screaming kids who must have thought we were the Beatles. They screamed through our entire set, much louder after each song, and I thought they would rush the stage when we finished our set. I doubt if any of them knew any of the songs we played, and probably very few had learned enough English to understand the words.

The curtain closed, and the auditorium became quiet as the kids were militarily marched out.

After our little bit of "Beatlemania", we had over a week before our next performance up in the DMZ at the Panmunjom service club, right next to the North Korean border. As usual, we spent the morning practicing with the General's Chorus, the afternoons practicing old and new songs, and the evenings stoned out of our heads and listening to Jimi Hendrix and Moby Grape on our headphones until long after midnight.

And at midnight, some of us who could still walk, would sneak over to the post bakery where the Korean bakers would give us a dozen freshly made glazed donuts. We'd skarf down our zuzus as soon as we got to our hootch.

This went on for the next week, and then...

Special Services supplied vans or busses whenever we needed transportation to gigs. The busses were well maintained since they were used all the time. However, the vans were old (no seat belts) and barely ran. Whenever we had to travel to bases around Second Division and I Corps, we were usually given a well-used Ford Econoline van. It had only two seats in it, and with five of us traveling, one person sat on the engine compartment, and two others sat on speaker boxes in the back. Our sound/light man, who was also our roadie, drove, and we took turns sitting in the passenger seat.

For gigs in the DMZ, the driver was issued a pistol—just in case. (We musicians weren't allowed to check out guns.) There were constant rumors of occasional sniper attacks and mines dug into the dirt roads. We heard that North Koreans snuck across the border and that South Koreans did the same, all for spying on troop movements. Those rumors seemed a little more real when we once did a gig at a MASH unit and saw a few of our own with wounds they got playing soldier around the DMZ.

It was mid-November, and the weather was getting cold. We were scheduled to play at a small service club in Panmunjom next to the Peace Center, which straddles the 38th Parallel, the border separating North and South Korea.

Gary, our driver/sound man/light man, signed out the same old black Ford van we had used several times before and pulled it up by the rehearsal hall. We had it loaded in less than thirty minutes and headed on our way north.

The trip took nearly an hour on dirt roads that ran up, over, and through innumerable hills and valleys. We were stopped for ten minutes at a checkpoint by the entrance to the DMZ as MPs checked and re-checked our papers and our gear. We were stopped again at the entrance to the Peace Center grounds and were checked all over again.

Our van had been sputtering and smoking quite a bit on the way to the gig, and barely made it up some of the steeper hills. We made it to the Peace Center. A couple of us expressed worry about getting stuck on the road going back.

When we finally pulled up by the service club, we had a little over an hour and a half to set up to play. We were scheduled to play two forty-five-minute sets, starting at 1900 hours (7:00pm) when it was still light out. We made a fast trip to the mess hall for a quick meal and then went back to finish setting up.

Since it was November, the sun had set behind the mountains by the time we started playing. By then, thousands of security lights had come on, both sides of the border, giving the entire complex an eerie bright blue glow that made the place look cold and stark. The outside air was getting colder by the minute, giving us a sampling of the winter to come.

We played two 45 to 50-minute sets to the hundred or so U.S. soldiers, CIA, and CID personnel, ROK army, and KATUSAs. All the U.S. people had a great time singing along with familiar songs, shouting and clapping. The Koreans barely smiled but clapped respectfully. It was hard to tell if they enjoyed themselves at all.

As usual, after we finished, we were inundated with questions and comments. ("You were good. How about playing some Beatles/Rolling Stones/Grateful Dead…"?)

We couldn't hang around too long. We had to be out of the Peace Center and past the DMZ before 2200 (10:00pm), the DMZ curfew. We finally had the van loaded by nine thirty, said our goodbyes to the few guys who helped us load up, and started the engine. Or rather, Gary tried to start the engine.

With the battery sounding like it was about dead, the engine finally started, and we drove away down the dirt road into the darkness outside the gate.

It was two winding miles over several hills to the ImJim River bridge. The van started sputtering again, like it was about to die, but Gary kept pumping the gas to keep it going. Unfortunately, when the first hill came up, the van couldn't make it with all five of us inside. The four of us band members got out and pushed the van up the hill as Gary strained to keep the van running. We all jumped back in the van as it started to pick up speed going downhill then made it nearly up the second hill just from momentum. We jumped out and pushed again.

The sky lit up. The sky exploded! We froze.

Artillery shells flew overhead. We couldn't tell whether they were from our side or theirs… or both.

We yelled at Gary to gun the engine as we pushed. When the van made it over the top, we made our best stunt man leaps into the moving vehicle. Gary stepped on it, and we got up to 40 miles per hour going downhill.

One more hill to climb.

We almost made it to the top. Out we jumped. We pushed. More explosions. We pushed harder. We leapt back in. The DMZ gate was just ahead along with a much flatter road beyond.

The guard on duty stopped us on return and we again had to show papers, even though he was the same one who let us in hours ago. With some artillery fire still going on, the guard didn't seem fazed by it. He had his duty, and come Hell or high water, he was going to do it.

He finally opened the gate and we chugged our way out of the DMZ and over the ImJim river. Only a couple more miles to go.

The few hills on the way weren't very high and the old van barely made it over them, but it did, and we made it back before curfew. Exhausted.

By the time we unloaded at the rehearsal hall and walked back to our hootch, we were too tired to stay up and listen to music and even too tired to toke. My head hit the pillow and I was out.

We found out a few days later that the artillery fire that night was practice rounds from our own artillery units. They fired shells that burst in the air, so they could, supposedly, determine the direction real rounds could be fired into the North Korean side of the DMZ. Still, it scared the hell out of us.

Through the Holidays, the chorus did a few Christmas themed events, not only for the General's Mess, but also for Korean orphans, where we sang *Silent Night* in Korean. The Travelers played gigs three and four times a week, with a New Year's Eve event at the RC #1 service club.

A few weeks later, the idea of a resurgence of the Korean conflict, and real live artillery rounds, became all too real.

Chapter 12
On Guard in the General's Chorus

Ugh. I'm not dreaming. This must be real. My eyes popped open, and I saw Top, the first sergeant, heading for me like a rampaging elephant. He grabbed my bunk with his huge hands and shook it until my blankets fell off. Then his big-footed, pot-bellied, six-foot frame thundered on to the next bewildered soldier and he did the same. Top was bedecked in full battle array, with a pack, his new M-16 rifle slung over his shoulder, and his ever-present 45 strapped to his hip. I rubbed my eyes and tried to focus. He yelled in his thick Georgia accent something about Commies.

I was cold. It was five o'clock in the morning on January 24, 1968. I wanted to pull my blankets back up, but Top had dropped my bunk down on top of them. The two diesel-fired space heaters weren't on. They had run out of fuel sometime in the middle of the night, and, because of the nightly curfew, our Korean houseboys wouldn't return to refill and relight them until noon. Outside, it was still a half hour until first light, and it was fifteen below zero. Inside in our uninsulated, steel-walled, corrugated metal-roofed, hootch, it was about the same. I wanted to get back under my blankets.

Top ordered us to put on our helmets and meet on the small parade ground in front of the company office. I had trouble keeping my eyes open, even with all of Top's yelling going on, but I heard him coming back on another run through the barracks and it sounded like he was turning bunks over to rouse the stragglers. I quickly slid my long john covered body out of bed and set my bare feet onto the ice-cold concrete floor. I had no more trouble keeping my eyes open.

Military activity had increased in several Far East Asian countries during the winter I was there. The Communist presence in South-east Asia had been getting larger and bolder, and North Korea seemed caught in the momentum. They had increased hostile activities all along the border and sometimes into South Korea. Most of this happened rather quietly since the attention of the Western press and the resources were in Vietnam and Cambodia.

What finally got the attention of the press on Korea was when the Pueblo, a United States Naval vessel, sailed where it shouldn't have, and was captured by North Korea the day before my rude awakening by Top. This caused the combined U.S. and South Korean armed forces to get jumpy and everyone went on alert, cocking guns and aiming them in every direction, just waiting for the word to shoot.

And the "shoot" word was close to coming the day after, when thirteen North Koreans made it to Seoul and attempted to assassinate the South Korean president. They failed, and, in desperation, threw hand grenades into the crowds as they forced their way through the congested streets. They killed and wounded many civilians and some of the South Korean soldiers who were trying to capture them. Three of the North Koreans died holding on to their own live grenades and two others were executed on the spot. The rest disappeared into, and became part of, the city's congestion. Then they traveled north, following along the river that ran by RC#1, and headed right toward us.

My feet were freezing. My eyes stung. My mouth tasted like the bottom of a hash pipe, and my brain still felt like I was at the bottom of a hash pipe. My fingers were cold and numb. It took a lot of effort for me to pull my fatigues on over my cotton long-johns. It took a lot more effort to button up the fatigues. I did manage to blouse my pants into my boots but fumbled with the laces and finally tied knots instead of bows. I put on my olive-drab fatigue jacket and then pulled on my thick parka, with its fur-lined hood, over that. Then came wool glove liners and thick leather gloves, and finally, the helmet (helmet liner plus net-covered outer shell).

Top was running through the hootch yelling again. To avoid his anger, pushing and shoving, I got up and quickly shuffled out into the cold. I joined thirty-five other pairs of shuffling feet headed for the cold gravel of the company parade ground, which was too small for parading, and barely large enough for all of us to gather on.

Top beat us there and yelled some more. "Line up, gawd dammit, you lazy fuckin' bastards!"

We lined up in a semi-circle around him.

"Straighten' that fuckin' line. ATTEN…HUT!"

A few regular Army guys sprang to attention, as did Top. The rest of us kept scraping our feet and clapping our gloved hands together to try to keep warm. Lieutenant Bowman, our company commander, made his appearance. He looked my age but acted much older. He was a quiet man who wanted to live a quiet life, listening to classical music, not rock and roll. He didn't like commanding a bunch of rock and rollers and left that job to Top, who usually avoided us. However, the lieutenant was regular Army. He marched smartly and erect in perfect, straight lines and right angles up to Top and stood facing him. They both made perfect salutes, and Top went through the traditional ceremony of turning over the platoon to the company commander. Perfectly. (I always thought those guys must practice in front of their mirrors.) The ceremony ended with Top stepping back a couple of steps, and on my foot. I moved back and bumped into the guy behind me. He moved—and so on, and so on, and so on, until we were moving and bumping into each other, some accidentally, a lot on purpose just to rile Top. It did.

"STAND STILL, YOU FUCKIN' QUEERS!"

We quieted down. Top did an about face away from us, as did the lieutenant.

Out of thin air came reveille. I winced, as did most of us, when loud, static, sort-of-bugle-like sounds trembled out of a rusting cone-shaped loudspeaker. That loudspeaker barely clung to a decaying power pole only by its own speaker wire, which connected it to the company record player. When the music started, the company clerk double-timed out of the office and ran Old Glory up the flagpole. Lieutenant Bowman and Top saluted and watched the flag as it rose.

Reveille ended. The Lieutenant did a smart (perfect) about face.

"Men," he began in his normal high pitched, whiney-sounding voice. Our attention was elsewhere, like getting back into a warm bed. Several of us mumbled some "shits" and "fucks," and shuffled our feet around in the gravel some more. "Men," he tried again, lowering his voice over a half octave. "Stand at ease." We were already at ease.

"Yesterday, a U.S. Navy ship, the Pueblo, was captured by North Korea." This caught our attention, and we quieted down.

We knew relations were strained between North and South Korea, as always, and we all knew very well, and worried, that it wouldn't take much to start another "police action". We had heard from some of the soldiers we entertained that a lot more sniper activity was occurring around the DMZ, sending more victims to the MASH units. They also told us North Koreans were mining some of the roads up there, the very roads we had traveled on. And the big rumor was that Vietnam would escalate so much that the Koreas would get caught up in it.

Lieutenant Bowman continued : "And last night, thirteen North Koreans made their way to Seoul and tried to assassinate the South Korean president." I felt our worst fears were about to come true. Nearly the whole platoon groaned in unison. "Men, you are privileged to be members of the only full-time entertainment company in the U.S. Army. You were chosen for this duty because of your singing talent and your ability to entertain. However, you are first and foremost soldiers. And since we are affiliated with the second infantry division, when worse comes to worst, you are" …pregnant pause, "…infantrymen."

More "shits" and "fucks" from the ranks, and a loud "shut the fuck up" from Top.

Infantry? I thought. I was trained as a clerk typist! Fuck!

The lieutenant continued. "I've been notified that Second Division, in fact all of Sixth Army Command, is on alert. There will be no, I repeat, no, travel permitted outside this compound. This means no entertaining, no performances, no… rock and roll. You are restricted here until notified otherwise by me. If you've already received passes, forget it. They're all revoked."

We were all silent now. In shock. It was like hearing that the world was going to end. And in a way, the world we knew seemed to be ending. The lieutenant looked us over, sighed, took a deep breath, and said, "So take a look at yourselves. The person you last saw in the mirror was a performer. The person you'll see now is an infantryman. The First Sergeant has already put together a duty roster, and the first shift will be pulling guard duty by 0800 hours. Sergeant?"

"ATTEN…HUT!" More snappy saluting, and the lieutenant turned us back over to Top, marched off the field and into his quarters. Top did an about face and looked us over from one end to another. A thin, tight-lipped smile spread across his face.

"Several North Korean commies escaped capture in Seoul," Top hissed, talking softly and slowly but quite clearly and without his usual drawl. It was more frightening than when he yelled. "There may be as many as eight of 'em. Our sources tell us that these Commies are headed our way and may be following that river over there back north." The river Top pointed to was around 50 feet wide, rocky, and very shallow, as well as mostly frozen over. It flowed along the entire length of our compound as it headed north to the canyon of the much larger Imjim river, right in the middle of the DMZ. "We'll all be on the lookout for these gooks, and if we see 'em, we'll capture 'em or kill 'em, God willing." Did I see a glint in Top's eyes? "I'm posting guards—you guys—by the front gate, behind the bakery, behind the PX, behind the bowling alley, and by the football field. You'll each rotate four-hour shifts—four hours on and four hours off—until we kill 'em, or..." pause, "this alert is over. All right, you assholes…uh, you soldiers, when you fall out, go to the mess and get your breakfast. By 0630, be back here, dressed for combat duty, and I'll march you all to supply for your weapons. Dis-s-s-smissed."

Yes, I was in shock, as were most of the others. We didn't move. I just stared blankly at the wall in front of us. I was numbed by the cold and by the thought of being in real gun battles. Here I was thinking I'd gotten out of combat by getting sent to Korea instead of Vietnam. Now I envisioned myself on guard duty, quietly minding my own business, getting ambushed from behind and getting my throat cut by some slant-eyed, psychopathic, North Korean version of a Green Beret, and left lying in a pool of blood while watching the "yellow peril/red menace" swarm over the football field to take over our bowling alley, loot our PX, and rape our service club hostesses.

"Shit!" I forced out of my clenched teeth. Next to me was my best friend, John, who also hadn't moved and was shivering and staring blankly at the wall.

"We should've burned our draft cards and gone to Canada," I told him.

"I enlisted."

"Huh?"

"I fucking enlisted. I was about to be drafted in '65, and this recruiting sergeant told me and my friend that if we enlisted, we'd get to choose our job and go someplace neat…like Germany." John's voice drifted off.

"Huh?"

"Huh? Oh. We enlisted. Asked to be radio operators, then got sent to Fort Sill for artillery training. The rumor was we were all going to Vietnam. I somehow got sent here instead. What pisses me off is that we were lied to. The fuckin' Army lied to us and got us to sign up for three years instead of the two we'd have gotten by getting drafted…like you." John's voice drifted off again and he sighed. "Fuck. Let's go eat."

After breakfast, before we got our guns, we went back to the hootch to think about what might happen next. We needed music, and pot, for our thoughts. I opened my "kimchee" cabinet and put the new *Sergeant Pepper's Lonely Hearts Club Band* album on at a decent, loud, level, then sat down on the edge of my bunk. I rolled a joint and lit it. The end of my tour of duty seemed so far away. John came over and sat down beside me, and I passed the joint to him.

That early morning our barracks were an unfamiliar bustle of chaotic activity. Everyone yelled, swore, smoked pot earlier than usual, and tried to put together combat gear some of us had never been issued and others had sold to the local black market or thrown away. Most of us made do with what little we had. Top's voice was easily heard over the cacophony. "AWLRIGHT MEN! TIME TA FAWL OUT!"

I extinguished the joint by pinching the end and put the remainder in my film-canister stash container and stuck it in my pocket. John and I looked at each other, sighed, got up, and meandered back out to the parade ground. When the platoon was nearly lined up, Top started bellowing orders. Attention. Left face. Forward march. To the right. March. Etcetera march. Did he notice we were just plodding along behind him, whispering to each other, wondering what was in store for us?

Top lined us up in front of the supply building, and the company clerk handed us all rifles—but no ammunition. (The rumor was that Top was afraid of being shot by his own men.) That was the first gun I'd had in my hand since basic training and

AIT, nearly a year earlier. We marched, or rather walked back to the parade ground where Top read the duty roster. Those scheduled for guard duty were paired up, so there would be two guards at each post. Somehow, John and I got assigned together for the two a.m. to six a.m. shift, the coldest and darkest hours of the night. Those not scheduled for guard duty, around a dozen guys, were the quick-reaction team. They were to be prepared for action at any time, day or night. If a guard post sighted any intruders, it was the team's job to chase, capture, and/or kill them (which would have been hard to do when Top had the only bullets).

We stood there for nearly fifteen minutes in the still freezing cold while Top delivered a fire and brimstone sermon on our God-given duty to protect our way of life from heathen Communists. He preached about our responsibilities as guards, and he evangelized about fending off surprise attacks. In that fifteen minutes he covered everything from love of God and mom's apple pie to hand-to-hand combat and how to use a bayonet most effectively.

When Top finally dismissed us, except for those who had to pull the first guard duty, John and I snuck over to the PX snack bar to get a couple of hamburgers (post-pot hunger) only to find that Lieutenant Bowman had ordered everything closed for the duration. No snacks, no movies, no service club, no bowling alley. Nothing. Hungry and unhappy, we returned to the hootch, got a bag of Ritz crackers and a can of tuna out of our lockers, and scarfed them down.

The day and evening passed with anxiety-ridden quickness. I tried reading to pass the time, but my mind was racing, making up battle scenarios, and wondering if I'd live through the night. I dozed off about midnight.

Top, who never seemed to sleep, shook John and me from our dopey slumbers at a quarter to two and marched us through the dark to our stakeout: the football field. I think the two guards we replaced were dozing. We were nearly upon them when they both jumped up with a yelp. One dropped his gun, and the other spun around so fast with his rifle and fixed bayonet that he nearly put a permanent grin on Top's face. Top quickly stepped back, bumping me into John, who nearly fell down.

"At ease, soldier," Top told the now extremely nervous guard. Top then clenched his teeth and sternly added, "You were supposed to challenge us, boy. You were supposed to yell, 'WHO GOES THERE.'" We all jumped when he yelled that. "You better not have been dozin' out here, or you'll have hell to pay. You all seen or heard anythin'?"

"No… n-nothing," they both stuttered. "J… just the river ice cracking once in a while. Can we go now? We're freezing."

John and I switched places with the guards. Top saluted us, reminded us to call if we heard anything, told the other two to fall in and marched them away. I looked at John. He looked at me. We looked at the others fading into the inky, cold, darkness, and we both sighed, emitting clouds of fog through our mouths. For the next four hours John and I had to watch and listen and keep from being killed or freezing to death.

Nothing in our compound was more remotely located from everything than the football field. It was separated from the rest of the compound by a large concrete ditch, about ten feet across and six feet deep, that flowed into the river behind us. That ditch, and the small wooden footbridge over it, separated us all too well from the safety and warmth of our beds.

Our job was to patrol along the chain-link fence behind the visiting team's bleachers, right next to the ice-covered river. On the other side of the river we could barely make out a few dim lights shining in farmhouse windows. Just beyond lay frozen rice paddies, snow-topped mountains, and darkness.

John and I were nervous, paranoid, and slightly stoned, which seemed to increase our alertness in a paranoid sort of way many times over. Noises seemed to come from every direction, always somewhere just past the perimeter of our night-vision. We heard noises that sounded like bloodthirsty Reds sneaking up to pounce on us. We heard noises that could be clips of ammo being slipped into rifles. We heard noises that could be bayonets snapping into place on rifle barrels.

We sat down on the first row of the bleachers, huddled close together for warmth, lit up the remainder of a joint, and spoke in whispers.

"John?" Toke.

"Yeah?"

"Did you hear that?" I handed the joint to John.

"What...what?" Toke. Toke.

"Doesn't it sound like someone's walking out there?"

"I don't hear anything. I don't want to hear anything."

"Come on. Listen. (Hand me the fuckin' joint!)"

A minute and the joint passed.

Crack.

"There!" I shouted, pointing to the river, the joint grasped between my thumb and index finger, and glowing brightly in the breeze. My voice scared both of us. I whispered, "Ah, jeez. Sh-h-h. Sorry. D'you hear that?"

"Oh shit. Oh shit. I think I did."

"L…listen. God, it sounds like someone sneaking around out there."

"Christ. Keep it down. Don't let them know we're here. Put that joint out."

We waited and listened.

Crack. Crack.

"Oh Christ! Oh shit!" I nearly yelled again. "They're all over the place."

"C'mon Ron, shut up. They'll hear you."

"D…do you think we should check it out?"

"With what. Top didn't give us any ammo. The goddam asshole's got the only bullets in the compound. I'm not going out there with just a bayonet. Let's call the quickie squad."

A small box next to the bleachers contained a phone left over from the recent football games. Top had told us to use it if we saw anything or needed help from the quick-reaction team. We felt we needed help, so John opened the box, lifted the phone off the hook, and cranked the handle. The noise exploded through the silence and startled us. Top answered.

"Headquarters. Sergeant Williams speakin'."

John covered the phone's mouthpiece and turned to me. "Sergeant Williams. Who the hell's Sergeant Williams."

"That's Top. Sergeant Bill Williams. You didn't know?"

"Shit no. I've only heard him called Top."

"What the fuck you guys want?" We heard yelled through the receiver.

John took his hand off the phone and stammered, "Uh, uh, this is John"

"What guard post is this?" Top yelled. John pulled the phone away from his ear.

"Uh, post 3. We need help."

"Roger. On our way."

John hung up the phone and closed the call box lid.

Five minutes later we saw our quick-reaction trained killers, following Top, in full battle regalia, and Lieutenant Bowman, with his pajama tops peeking out of his thick coat, double timing across the football field toward us.

"Think we should challenge them?" John asked me.

"Maybe we'd better. I really don't want Top yelling at us more than usual."

"You do it."

"Me! It's been over a year since I pulled guard duty. What do I do?"

"Just yell halt," John whispered.

"Yell what? I can't hear you."

"Yell halt."

"What?"

"HALT!"

Top, Lieutenant Bowman, and the quick-reaction team came to a noisy stop, rifles, packs, and helmets all clattering together.

"Uh," John stammered, as I turned away chuckling to myself. "Uh… who goes there?"

"You know who the fuck we are, ass… soldier!" Top yelled but quieted down quickly at the lieutenant's prodding.

I turned back around to face Top and the others, barely able to keep a straight face, with my rifle and bayonet pointed straight at Top's face. "Advance to be recognized."

You could almost hear the pressure building up inside the sergeant as he slowly came toward us, raising his rifle up to my face. Realizing he had bullets and I didn't, I made a hasty retreat. "Um… you're recognized. Proceed."

Top proceeded right up to my ear; his rifle almost buried in my armpit.

"What you boys got out there?" Top whispered through clenched teeth, hissing hot air into my ear. He pulled out his bayonet and mounted it on his rifle, which still felt like it was in my armpit, and took his pistol out of its holster in what seemed like one quick move. "Have them gooks showed up for us to exterminate?"

Top's voice went from anger to a sort of psychotic excitement, words from hot to icy cold. I shivered. I could barely see him next to me in the darkness, but I saw his eyes were wide and seemed to sparkle, and I was sure I saw a glint of saliva trickling down from the corners of his mouth. In my stoned state, I started rattling off the first thing that came into my head, impersonating Top, whispering through clenched teeth and all.

"I don't know, Top, but it sure sounds like there's several gooks out there on the ice. I thought we heard talking," I lied. "What you want us to do?"

"You men keep your position here. My contingent and me will reconnoiter the perimeter. If we make contact with the hostiles, you all circle around the periphery and encounter them from the opposite side. The Lieutenant will call in and report our operations to headquarters."

"Huh?" John and I chorused in unison. Hearing Top speak words with more than one syllable shocked both of us. We looked at each other and shrugged. Top was in his element.

"Don't you all worry none now," Top whispered in my ear, leaning into me, his rifle finding its way into my armpit again. "I got this shit under control." I leaned away.

He swung his arm around motioning for the men to fan out. None of them were paying attention to him, they were huddled together on the team bench, behind us on the fifty-yard line, trying to keep warm. Without saying a word, Top reached back and tapped his rifle barrel on several of their helmets. He pointed to those he tapped and waved them off to our left. He pointed to the others and waved them off to our right. Top kept flashing his rifle and waving his pistol threateningly in their direction, so they quickly split up and crawled along the fence in both directions away from us. The sudden flurry of activity startled the Lieutenant out of his slumber. He was sitting on the bench on the other side of us and had nodded off. He straightened himself up like he was trying to stretch the kinks out of his back. "Shit," was all we heard him say, very quietly and to no one. He pulled his collar up around his ears, pulled his helmet down tighter on his head, folded his arms, leaned back across a couple of bleachers, and stared off over the football field. His breath created an occasional cloud of steam as it mingled with the cold air.

No steam, however, escaped from Top's mouth. He seemed to be holding his breath. I guessed so he could hear better. His head jerked from side to side like he was trying to determine the location of every little sound, and he seemed to tremble. I couldn't tell if it was from the cold or from itchy-trigger-fingered anticipation.

My mind was beginning to clear. John and I were both coming down from our pot-induced paranoia and were feeling more at ease, especially with everyone out there with us. I wondered if all we heard was the shifting of the river's ice, like the other guards said. However, I wasn't about to tell Top or Lieutenant Bowman my thoughts. We felt much more comfortable with them around, at least at that moment.

Less than fifteen minutes later the others returned and reported to Top.

"There's nothin' out there. We didn't see anything."

"We thought we heard something, but we didn't see anything either. It's just the ice crackin' or something."

"Let's get the fuck out of here and back where it's warm."

"It's fuckin' freezing."

"Fuckin' place."

"Shit!"

"Fuck!"

Lieutenant Bowman stood up and started to leave. "C'mon Top, let's go. Uh, Top?"

Top was staring across the river into the blackness.

"Top?" Lieutenant Bowman asked again.

"Someone's out there, sir." Top whispered, still straining to see anything in the dark. "I hear them. I smell them. I know they're there. I know they's just on the other side of the river."

"Top. Leave it. Let's go. The guards will call us if anyone shows up, won't you guys."

Top stood up very slowly and did a 360° turn surveying as much as he could, rifle in one hand, pistol in the other, both extended out in front of him, ready to fire.

He put his pistol back in its holster, unmounted and sheathed his bayonet, and cradled his rifle in his arms, his right hand still resting on the trigger.

Top turned to us. "I can feel it. I know those fuckin' Reds are out there. You men keep a sharp lookout and call me if you see 'em. And don't fuck with me when I come back." Top started to leave then turned to us again. A weird grin crossed his lips and he said through clenched teeth, "Don't take all the glory, I want to be in on the kill."

Yeah, right. With an empty rifle and a bayonet. Another shiver ran through me, and it wasn't due to the cold.

They left.

John and I had a couple more hours of guard duty remaining. Sometime during all the commotion, I lost the joint, and we spent most of the remaining time trying to find it. We were cold, sober, and getting scared again. We sat as close together as possible to keep warm, with our rifles lying on the ground, disregarding all the snaps, cracks, and pops coming from the river.

For the next week everything continued in the same nerve-racking manner as that first night. Political and military turmoil was the order of the day, and rumors, all bad, were spreading around our compound fast and furiously. Even though we felt we were in the middle of it all, we weren't the only ones affected. All the GI's in South Korea, and, I'm sure, our counterparts in North Korea, were nervous about the possibility of a bloody encounter. Both countries pointed fingers and guns and were very close to another full-scale war. The United States threatened to invade North Korea to rescue the Pueblo crew. Border skirmishes increased and occasional shots rang out each night as soldiers fired at anything that moved or made a noise. South Korean soldiers stole north to snipe and plant mines. North Korean soldiers stole south to do the same Both sides blew up taxis, buses, and people. Occasionally they actually hit a military target. The hospitals filled up. Several guys in our barracks smuggled in a kilo of grass and two prostitutes so several of them could pass this war in comfort.

And across the river from us a South Korean farmer was killed by the infiltrators when he caught them stealing food from his pantry… that very night we were on guard in the General's Chorus.

Epilogue

The General's Chorus pulled guard duty barely three days during the Pueblo incident. Even though the Pueblo crew was confined in North Korea, the remaining infiltrators were all caught trying to sneak back across the border. The powers that be cancelled the alert and business went back to normal.

Normal? Because Chuck's alter ego was a Swiss Army sergeant with his uniform and beret to match and dog tags that said, "Le Armée Suisse" and "Charlemagne Mosher" and because he claimed he was a United Nations soldier and constantly spoke in a French accent, Top believed him. Chuck never had to pull guard duty like the rest of us.

Normal? Allison kept up his double-jointed gargoyle act and Top left us alone. Top left Korea a few weeks after the alert. His replacement hated being on a recreation compound and spent most of his time in the village. We hardly saw him.

Normal? The bands played on.

I went on one tour with the variety show and four tours of Korea with the Travelers. We got to be tourists in Taegu and visited a Buddhist monastery where I purchased a prayer bead bracelet and necklace. Each had a "peep show" bead with a tiny image of Buddha in it. I picked up a book on Buddhism and started practicing once we returned to RC#1. I even had new dog tags made in the village that proved I was Buddhist. I wore my beads with my uniform. Unfortunately, I lost them when home.

My last band tour of Korea in early Fall 1968 was as an advisor, helping to train my bass-playing replacement. It was getting close to time for me to get out of the army, and after we got back to the hootch, I started packing up my stereo and records, so I could ship them home. For my last few weeks in Korea, I did nothing but read, listen to music on other stereos, go bowling, print photos in the base photo lab, and smoke a lot of boo.

My last day in Korea was spent back at Camp Ross, where I first started out. After the final indignity of being forced to get a drastic butch-top haircut, I sat around for an army bus to arrive and take me and several other soldiers to the airport for the 13-hour flight back to the Seattle-Tacoma airport. From there it was a bus ride to Fort Lewis for two days of hanging around for the out-processing procedures.

Once I got my papers and final pay, I was officially a civilian again. I called my parents and told them I was coming home.

A lot had happened in the two years I played soldier. When I was drafted, I was a folk-singing cowboy with four horses. By the time I had returned, I was a professional musician. Uncle Sam had taught me how to rock and roll. The horses were gone, and I never got back in the saddle again.

But, as an ex-draftee, I was supposed to be a reservist and go to Army Reserve campouts each Summer for two years, with the possibility of being re-inducted if more war, or rather, police action, escalated in southeast Asia. I refused to have anything to do with the Army and had burned my uniforms shortly after I got home. I wrote to our local congressman, a staunch anti-war politician, to make sure I was excused from having to serve again. His support kept me from ever getting a visit by the military police.

While I was in Korea, both Jack Kerouac and Neal Cassidy had died. Robert Kennedy and Martin Luther King had been assassinated.

I had missed out on Monterey Pop and the Summer of Love. What I resolved not to miss out on was starting a new band.

That band, Throckmorton, was formed by several of us who had been in Korea together. It became very popular in the San Francisco Bay area, once backing Chuck Berry and playing at the Fillmore. Our band commune in San Jose was a gathering place for some Doobie Brothers and future Fleetwood Mac members, and our house had originally been the site of some of Ken Kesey's acid tests. I married my fiancée and eventually became a carpenter, just like my dad, living my version of the All-American dream.

It's been well over 50 years since these events took place. The main subjects in this series of reminiscences are true, but it is possible some of my grey cells have been lost. Where my memory has failed, I made use of my artistic license. I just hope it doesn't get revoked.

Photo Gallery

The following photos show key moments that took place in my life. There are no photos from my eight weeks in basic training since I did not have a camera while there. The few I took at Fort Ord are too blurry to use. I took most of these photos with a Polaroid Swinger that I got as a Christmas present that took only 2" x 3" black and white photos, a 16mm Japanese pocket camera I purchased while in Japan, and a Japanese Pentax 35mm camera I bought at the RC#1 PX.

1: 1965-Once I was a Cowboy…

2: …and a Folk Singer

3:1967-After 16 weeks of training, I'm now a Soldier in Oklahoma

4: 1967-Oklahoma Folk Trio in Concert

5: September 1967-Korea-Camp Ross Entrance

6: September 1967-My Desk in the Camp Ross S1 Security Office

7: September 1967-Security Field Training

8: September 1967-Driving the Sergeant Major to see his Yobo

9: November 1967-Arrival at RC#1

10: November 1967-Singing in the Variety Show

11: January 1968-Practicing my new Bass

12: December 1967-The Travelers Ready to Board the Train to Pusan

13: Spring 1968-Cleaned and Pressed Uniform

14: Summer 1968-Soldier Totem

15: Summer 1968-No Smoking

16: Summer 1968-I've Always Read a Lot

138

17: Yonjugol

18: Yonjugol Street Market

19: Yonjugol-The "Turkey Farm"

20: Outside Yonjugol-Delivering Wood

140

Author's Notes

This revised 2nd edition fills in some blanks in my memories. After both my editor (wife) and my re-reading it, the redlines added too much color to the pages and needed to be taken care of. Corrections included fixing the timeline in a couple of the stories and some spelling and formatting glitches here and there.

RC#1 wasn't the only recreation compound in Korea. It was the first of four compounds in the 2nd Division and I-Corps that stretched across the northern part of South Korea at that time. All are now closed and the temporary buildings are finally all gone. Also closed are quite a few of the U.S. Army bases in Korea. The ones north of Seoul and closer to the DMZ are still quite active.

Now, about the music of that era. In 1966-1968, it was new and exciting to a young rock and rolling bass player. In the variety show group and the Travelers, some of the music played was by The Jefferson Airplane (*Somebody to Love*), Moby Grape (*Listen My Friends, Hey Grandma*), The Association (*Windy, Cherish, Along Comes Mary*, The Nashville Teens (*Tobacco Road*), Cream (*Sunshine of Your Love, White Room*), and The Fortunes (*You've Got Your Troubles*). There were more, but memory fails me.

Recorded music was played on several record players throughout the two buildings everyone lived in, sometimes through speakers, but most often through headphones. Surprisingly, I didn't ruin my ears listening to Jimi Hendrix, Cream, and the Beatles (*Sergeant Pepper*) at high volume through my headphones. Of course, after playing in loud rock bands for seven plus years and being a carpenter in heavy construction for a dozen years, some of my hearing might be a little less than normal.

(Huh? What'd you say?)

Biography

Ron Cook is an author, artisan luthier and craftsman living in Santa Cruz, California. He has appeared in, and written for, Renaissance Magazine, and his works have appeared in American Woodworker, American Craft, Early Music America, Dulcimer Players News, Crafts Report, Guitarmaker, Sunset, and several technical trade journals. He and his works have appeared on television: WABC in New York, KGO in San Francisco, San Jose Community TV, and Community Television of Santa Cruz. Ron has also written five books… so far.

As a craftsman, he uses sustainably harvested, salvaged, and urban forest woods to create one-of-a-kind medieval and Early American stringed instruments, furnishings and sculptures. Distinctive carvings, often known for their subtle humor, are the hallmark of his works and include figures researched from history and legend, as well as from subjects observed in daily life.

Ron exhibited nationally at American Craft Council Shows and many art and craft festivals for many years. His pieces have been shown in galleries and events as far away as Barcelona, Spain, and are in collections throughout the world.

Ron is a 50+-year member of the Guild of American Luthiers and was a Santa Cruz County Open Studios artist for 20 years. He is also a member of the Mystery Writers of America and Sisters in Crime. He also belongs to and supports the National Music Museum in Vermillion, South Dakota.

www.ingramcontent.com/pod-product-compliance
Lightning Source LLC
Chambersburg PA
CBHW020544160726
47991CB00002B/573